More Lakeland Walking: On the Level

Norman Buckley

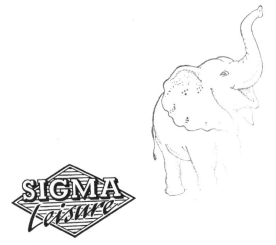

Published by Sigma Leisure – an imprint of
Sigma Press, 1 South Oak Lane, Wilmslow, Cheshire SK9 6AR, England.

British Library Cataloguing in Publication Data
A CIP record for this book is available from the British Library.

ISBN: 1-85058-572-5

Typesetting and Design by: Sigma Press, Wilmslow, Cheshire.

Cover photograph: Landing Stage on Windermere (June C. Buckley)

Photographs: Norman Buckley

Maps: Elizabeth Fowler

Printed by: MFP Design and Print

Disclaimer: the information in this book is given in good faith and is believed to be correct at the time of publication. No responsibility is accepted by either the author or publisher for errors or omissions, or for any loss or injury howsoever caused. Only you can judge your own fitness, competence and experience.

Preface

"Lakeland Walking on the Level", published three years ago, has quite obviously fulfilled the objectives stated in its preface and that of the companion "Yorkshire Dales Walking on the Level". The author's belief that there are many walkers and potential walkers who enjoy walking in the Lake District, but for whatever reason are unable and/or do not wish to climb the hills and mountains which dominate the great majority of other walking guides, has been borne out by the popularity of the book.

It is now apparent that many "level" walkers have tried out virtually all the original routes; hence this second volume of more of the same thing. As before, many walks are in the heart of the District, in close proximity to the great mountains, which can be admired from these routes without the immense effort required for an ascent. Equally, "fringe" areas such as the Winster valley, Askham and Shap, where the more gentle terrain lends itself admirably to this format, are explored.

In these books the term "level" is not, of course, to be interpreted literally. It means that great care is taken to limit the overall ascent to the minimum and that the length and severity of individual rises within a route and conditions underfoot are also taken into account in deciding whether or not a walk qualifies for inclusion. The introduction to each walk quantifies the length, the rise and fall, and briefly describes the route in such a way that its suitability for any particular circumstances can be very quickly assessed. Other introductory information recommends car parking places and appropriate maps. Whilst any route can be followed with total reliability from the text and the sketch maps provided, there is no doubt that the use of a map such as those of the Ordnance Survey Outdoor Leisure series adds greatly to the appreciation of the surrounding countryside.

Because "level" walking is expected to be a leisurely process, there is a brief description of features of interest along the way and refreshment opportunities are mentioned.

In Lakeland it has always been true to say that for maximum comfort, protection and safety, boots should always be worn, even on the shortest and easiest of these walks. Observation of the basic country code, particularly with regard to dogs and to closing of gates, is likewise important.

Norman Buckley

Contents

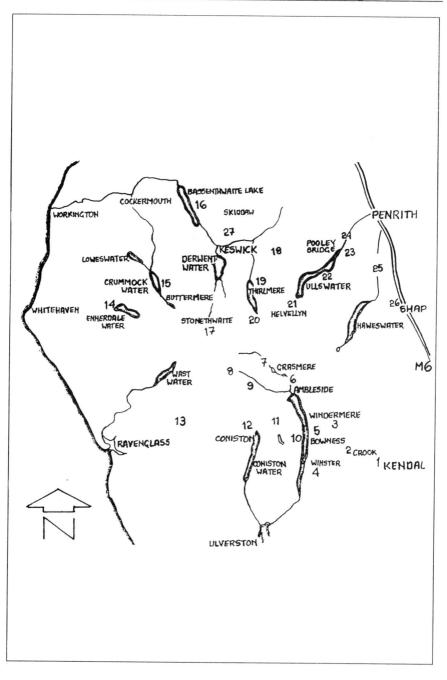

1. Cunswick Scar, Kendal

Length: 3¼ miles

Rise and Fall: Approximately 400 feet (122 metres), mainly in two sections. Firstly, close to the start and latterly in the rise from the by-pass to the top of the scar. No really steep gradients

Underfoot: No problems, although by no means all the public rights of way are marked on the ground. Particularly good along the top of the scar. Half a mile along the side of the Crook Road at the end of the walk.

Car Parking: Good sized lay-by on the Windermere to Kendal road (A5284) 100 metres or so on the Kendal side of the huge roundabout. Grid reference 499945.

Map: Ordnance Survey Outdoor Leisure no. 7, The English Lakes, South Eastern area, 1:25,000 or Landranger no. 97, Kendal to Morecambe, 1:50,000.

Description

The outward route of this circuit is through farming countryside bisected by the main Kendal bypass road, with a return along the top of Cunswick Scar. The scar is part of the rim of limestone surrounding the older rocks which comprise the core of the Lake District. As with the better known Scout Scar, immediately to the south (ref. the author's "Lakeland Walking on the Level" – Sigma Press), a steep scarp, high in part, faces west. The resultant views over the upper reaches of the Lyth valley to the Lake District mountains are very fine indeed, ranging from the Coniston fells, Crinkle Crags, Bowfell and Langdale Pikes round to the mountains grouped above Kentmere. Much of the face of the scar is wooded and the views improve as progress is made along the top.

As in the case of Scout Scar, the botanical interest rests largely on the assortment of lime loving plants, rare or absent from the Lake District proper.

Route

Walk along the side of the road towards Kendal for a few metres, then turn right at a gate to pass through a tunnel under the roadway of the by-pass. Bear left along the obvious trackway, ascending steadily. Kendal Fell, largely occupied by the golf course, rises just beyond the bypass. Grayrigg Forest and the Howgill Fells are in view further to the east. Go straight through Helsfell Farm, and turn right 20 metres after the exit gate to head for a stile which shows as a gap in the wall at the top of the field. Angle left, aiming just to the right of two isolated stunted hawthorn trees. Two stiles, with yellow arrow, give access to the bridge which carries the path high over the by-pass.

At the far end of the bridge another ladder stile offers a choice of yellow arrows. Turn right to follow a footpath faintly marked on the ground, heading above the line of trees ahead. Just before a cattle grid turn right, over a high ladder stile, and go down the field, bearing a little left as the buildings of Boundary Bank are seen to the right, ahead. Go over a ladder stile at the bottom and carry on down an old lane, a little rough underfoot, to a gate.

Cross a farm access road to a path over cut grass and a stile. Cross the by-pass and ascend the steepish bank on the far side to a sign and a footpath diversion notice. Take the indicated line to a field boundary wall and turn left, uphill. Go over two stiles in quick succession and continue uphill past a post with yellow arrow to a stile over the wall ahead.

The way now lies over more open ground to the top of the scar, marked by a stone wall along the top of the scarp. A gap to the left of the trees gives a first prospect of the wonderful Lake District panorama which is such an important part of this walk. Just below are what appear to be the remains of a lime kiln.

Turn right to walk north along the limestone top, delightfully dry underfoot and with the views improving steadily as progress is made. In common with some other very modest heights, Cunswick Fell provides a fine viewing gallery. There is some up and down but gradients are nowhere steep.

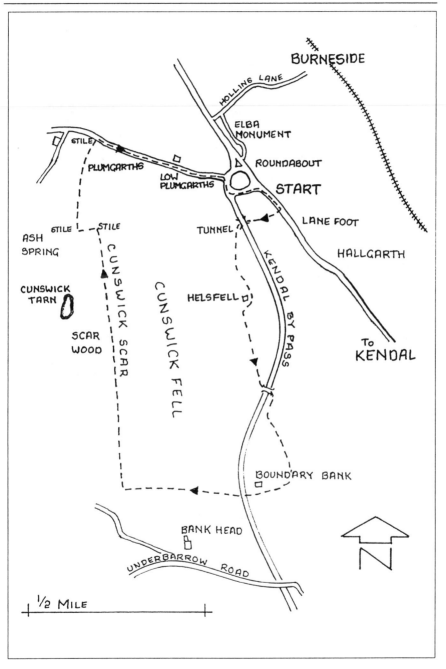

Cunswick Scar

At forks keep left, generally close to the top of the scarp, but ignore the signposted track on the left which descends through Scar Wood. After almost 1 mile reach an arrowed stile and turn left to another stile in a few yards. Cross a narrow field to yet another stile and turn hard right to follow a clear path along the top of the bank. Descend steadily through the edge of woodland, largely ash and hawthorn, with bramble undergrowth and some conifer planting.

Go over two more stiles and across the middle of a little meadow to a stile giving access to the Crook (Bowness to Kendal) Road. Turn right to return to the car parking lay-by.

```
┌─────────────────────────────────────────────┐
│  ┌───────────────────────────────────────┐  │
│  │                                       │  │
│  │            2. Crook                   │  │
│  │                                       │  │
│  └───────────────────────────────────────┘  │
└─────────────────────────────────────────────┘
```

Length: 3¾ miles (shorter version 2½ miles)

Rise and Fall: About 360 feet (110 metres) (shorter version 230 feet – 70 metres).

Underfoot: Generally good footpaths, but some not apparent on the ground, and 1¼ miles of surfaced road, mostly quiet minor road.

Car Parking: Small lay-by adjacent to the Sun Inn by the public telephone box. Grid reference 464952.

Map: Ordnance Survey Outdoor Leisure no. 7, The English Lakes, south eastern area, 1:25,000 or Landranger no. 97, Kendal to Morecambe, 1:50,000.

Description

A short walk in the attractive countryside around Crook at the head of the Lyth valley. Softer in character than central Lakeland, there are, nevertheless, rocky outcrops and sufficient elevation to provide fine views to the Lake District mountains and to the western fringe of the Pennines, well beyond Kendal.

Crook is a scattered settlement, with the Sun Inn as its most obvious focal point. The remains of the former St. Catherine's church stand forlorn on a knoll among fields. Only the tower of about 1620 now remains, the remainder having been declared unsafe and demolished in 1887.

Route

Walk along the road towards Bowness and turn left into a surfaced lane (Dobby Lane), soon rising a little to reach Old Mill Cottages, almost a hamlet. Continue to the end of the lane, cross a road and go over a stile in the wall opposite.

Cross a little stream and follow a path rising quite steeply over

The countryside around Crook

scrubby grassland towards the left hand edge of sparse woodland. Go through a kissing gate and keep well left of the woodland, the route not well marked on the ground. Behind there are good views across to the Pennine Hills.

Bear left to a ladder stile over the wall ahead. The countryside hereabouts is very attractive, with rocky outcrops. The tower of the abandoned church can be seen ahead. Aim a little to the left of this to reach the angle of two walls. Stay close to a wall on the left as far as another stile. Bear a little right to pass some outbuildings of Crook Hall, reaching a junction of several routes by farm gates.

Go through and take the obvious track straight to the former church. Immediately after the church the track turns right, angling down towards a wall on the left. The replacement church of 1887 is close below. At a three way signpost follow "public footpath Crook Road", reaching the road at a kissing gate.

Cross the road to go over a ladder stile, taking the direction across a meadow indicated by a finger post. Go through a gate

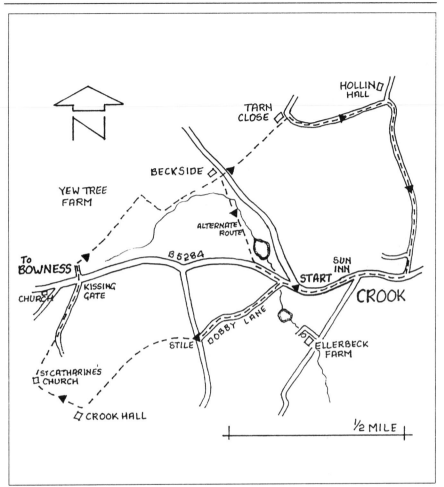

and continue the same line across the next meadow to a stile in the top left corner. Stay close to the wall on the left until a ladder stile with two yellow arrows is reached. Turn right before the stile to descend to a gate/stile in the bottom. There is some evidence here that walkers may be cutting the corner by heading directly to the gate/stile.

Turn left and head straight for Beckside alongside a bustling beck. After another gate a lane between stone walls goes to the farm, the outbuildings of which include a large bank barn.

(For the shorter walk turn right at a stile by the side of a stream just after the farm, head for a gate and return to the Bowness to Kendal road in less than half a mile. Turn left back to the car park)

Cross a minor road, ascend the bank by a Signpost "Tarn Close and Crook Road", go over a stile and keep close to the wall on the left for a steep climb of 120 feet (37 metres) or so.

Go over the stile at the top, through a kissing gate and carry on to Tarn Close with its modest pond, presumably the "tarn" of its title. Pass to the right of a fine old Lakeland outbuilding and bear right to take the surfaced access drive away from Tarn Close. There are more fine Pennine views as the drive descends to a minor road. Turn right and walk to the Bowness to Kendal road, half a mile distant. Turn right to return to the Sun Inn and car park.

3. Ings

Length: 4 miles (shorter version 3½ miles)

Rise and Fall: 430 feet (131 metres) in total, with 190 feet (52 metres) right at the outset on the surfaced lane up to Grassgarth.

Underfoot: Very good except for short lengths of rough farmland. About 50% on surfaced lanes.

Car Parking: Roadside spaces along cut off portion of former main road at Ings. Grid reference 445987.

Map: Ordnance Survey Outdoor Leisure no. The English Lakes, south east area, 1:25,000 or Landranger no. 97, Kendal to Morecambe, 1:50,000.

Description

A circuit among the farming countryside on both sides of the Kendal to Windermere main road (A 591). The rocks of the Silurian period, which fringe so much of the southern Lake District, underlie a landscape which is altogether softer and more rolling than is the case in the rocky "Borrowdale series" area at the core of the district. This landscape is undoubtedly attractive in its own right, particularly to "level" walkers and provides fine viewpoints for the more spectacular mountains.

Ings is a tiny village, totally overwhelmed by the proximity of the main road, with filling station and large roadside cafe. By the parking place, however, is the 18th. century parish church of St. Anne, the second church to be constructed on this site. St. Anne's has good carvings, a dated door lock from the previous church and an old choir gallery. Close by is the large and popular Watermill Inn.

The branch railway to Windermere was opened on 20th. April, 1847, a momentous day in the history of tourism in the Lake

District. Indeed, it could be argued that on that date mass tourism in the District truly began. Linked to what later became known as the West Coast main line at Oxenholme, this branch brought visitors by the hundreds of thousands eager to explore the wondrous beauty now accessible across a wide spectrum of society. In terms of building development of the Windermere/ Bowness/ Ambleside area it is also difficult to overstate the importance of the railway. The Manchester cotton magnates, now assured of rapid communication with the source of their wealth, built their splendid villas, most now converted to hotels, along the shore of the lake. Three local building firms worked flat out to construct the small town of Windermere, working downhill from the station towards the lake and to extend the ancient village of Bowness, ultimately as a lakeside resort. The great days of the railway have gone but the line, now single track, is thankfully still operational, of great benefit to both residents and visitors.

Near Ings

Route

Walk to the junction at the Windermere end of the cut off section of road and cross the main road to a surfaced lane directly opposite. Cross a bridge over a stream and rise steadily for almost 200 feet (61 metres) to Grassgarth, passing a 1953 ER II seat on the way. To the left the minor peaks of Grandsire and School Knott are in view, together with the upland area of Windermere Common.

Fork left to leave the surfaced road just after the main buildings of Grassgarth and follow a stony track across the front of St. Anne's Cottages. In a few yards turn left again, downhill. Turn right in 25 metres to a wooden footbridge and gate, with yellow arrow. Descend along the left side of a narrow meadow, cross a tiny stream and continue fairly close to the wall on the left. After some swampy ground cross the River Gowan on another footbridge, this time with gates.

Ascend a little and go through a farm gate to follow a level, terraced, grassy path. Go through another farm gate and turn left along a farm trackway to rise to a gate and surfaced roadway. Turn left. In 100 metres reach a minor public road at another gate and turn left. In 100 metres, just before Broadgate Farm, turn right at a signposted gate and keep to the edge of a triangular field. Go over a stile then keep a little left of the previous line to reach another stile over a fence and wall. The path hereabouts is hardly marked and the going is comparatively rough.

Heaning Farm is now in view. Aim well to the right of the buildings to a stile in the top left corner of the field. Turn left at the surfaced lane. To the left, Reston Scar above Staveley is well seen, backed by distant Pennine Hills on a clear day. Fork left in 100 metres on to an old lane, by passing Heaning Farm, and continue to the main road.

Go straight across to a gate and surfaced farm access road rising a little to cross the Windermere branch railway line. Stay with this roadway as it swings right then left to pass by Blackmoss before turning sharp left at a gate to head for Whasdike. Behind

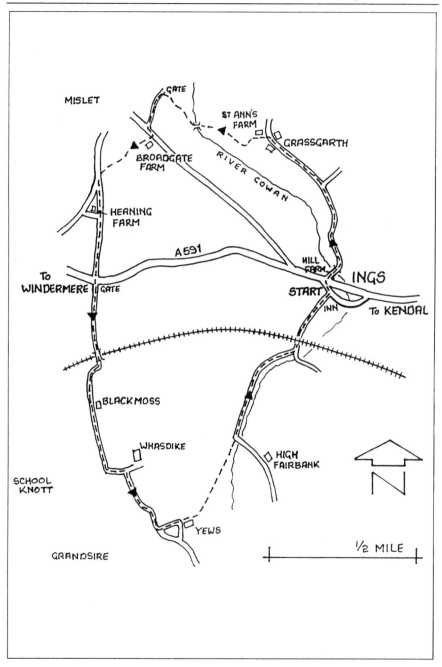

is a superb mountain panorama – Wetherlam, Crinkle Crags, Bowfell and the Langdale Pikes are all there. A triangular junction is soon reached. For the full circuit turn right, uphill.

(For the shorter version carry on to Whasdike and keep right of the buildings to follow a bridleway leading directly to the unfenced road above Ings)

In less than half a mile turn left, downhill, at the entrance drive to Yews. Go over the ladder stile to the left and continue downhill to a gate at the bottom of the field. There is no obvious path, but keep roughly to the middle of the open ground between groups of trees. Bend a little left to cross the next field, keeping right of the trees, to reach a small ladder stile.

Go over and stay roughly parallel with a small stream on the right to join an unfenced surfaced road. Turn left to return under the railway line to the car parking area, admiring the view of Red Screes towering over the Kirkstone Pass, away to the left.

4. Winster and Ghyll Head

Length: 3¾ miles

Rise and Fall: A total of approximately 530 feet (162 metres), of which about half is the ascent of the valley side early in the walk. The only other significant climb is through Spring Wood on the return to Winster. The gradients are reasonable in each case.

Underfoot: Most of the route is over very good footpaths. Less than half a mile on the road at the end of the walk.

Car Parking: Small unofficial lay-by on the A5074 (actually quite a minor road) at Winster. Grid reference 418937.

Map: Ordnance Survey Outdoor Leisure no. 7 The English Lakes, south eastern area 1:25,000 or Landranger no. 97, Kendal to Morecambe 1:50,000.

Description

The Winster valley is typical south Lakeland "Silurian" country-side, the geology giving rise to an altogether softer, more gentle landscape than the rocky "Borrowdale Volcanic" area of central Lakeland. The mixture of rolling hills and woodland is very attractive as walking country, not least because the area remains peaceful at times when Langdale and Borrowdale are full to capacity – an excellent choice for a Bank Holiday!

Those who believe that anywhere south of Bowness is flat land will be surprised. The total rise and fall is greater than might be expected on a comparatively short walk, but reasonable gradients and fine paths underfoot do help on these ascents. There are mountain and lake views along the way.

Winster is no more than a scattered hamlet with an unpretentious 19th. century church and the Brown Horse Inn which can, of course, play an important part in the enjoyment of the modest circuit.

Ghyll Head Reservoir

Route

From the lay-by walk south along the road to the Brown Horse. Turn right into the minor road signposted to Bowland Bridge and Winster church. Pass the farm at Green Yew and then turn right at a gate/stile with footpath sign, before reaching a belt of woodland. (*Winster church is a further a quarter of a mile along this road*)

Go along the edge of the field to a second gate/stile and descend gently by the edge of woodland with vegetation which is lush by Lakeland standards. Leave the wood at a stile and continue the same line close to a fence and old wall on the left to reach a small stream, actually the headwaters of the River Winster. Cross by a rather elaborate stone and concrete bridge and begin the long rise up the far side of the valley. At first the path is not obvious on the ground, but keep close to a wall on the right to reach a stile half concealed behind a rocky outcrop. Go over and cross a tiny field surprisingly planted with an arable crop, rare in these parts.

Go over a stile by a gate on the left and bear left along a farm type track to a kissing gate. A broad track now passes behind Birket Houses, along the foot of a steep wooded hillside. A surfaced road is reached at Winster House. Turn right, leave the road in 30 metres, and continue up the steepest part of the ascent, somewhat redeemed by the excellence of the path.

Emerge quite suddenly into more open countryside at a farm gate, pausing for breath and to admire the long views. Turn left for 20 metres along a farm track, then right at a post with yellow arrow. A narrow but always distinct path now weaves its way across about three quarters of a mile of this fine upland, with mountain views including the Coniston group, Crinkle Crags, Bowfell and the Langdale Pikes, unmistakable as ever. The path is superb underfoot and, despite Mr. Wainwright's sound advice on this subject, the view can be enjoyed whilst in motion without undue risk of falling over.

Ghyll Head Road is reached all too soon. Over the wall opposite is the reservoir of the same name, rather prettier than might be expected.

Retrace the path for 40 metres or so to start the more level of the two available routes to Rosthwaite Farm, our next objective. (*the alternative goes through the Access Land to the left*). Go through the kissing gate and along the bottom edge of the woodland, soon reaching plank bridges across a swampy area. As the two routes join at a kissing gate, keep straight on, over a stile, and look for a glimpse of Windermere.

At a junction with post and yellow arrows turn right for "Rosthwaite" (not to be confused with its more famous namesake in Borrowdale). Another broad, easy track descends to the farm, in view ahead. Unusually for a farm, the whole complex is beautifully flower-bedecked in summer. The adjacent ornamental pond has several varieties of water fowl.

Pass through and turn right immediately after the farm, at a gate/stile with a "Winster" footpath sign. A wide tack rises through the conifers of Spring Wood, soon steepening to provide the second significant ascent of the walk. At the top is another

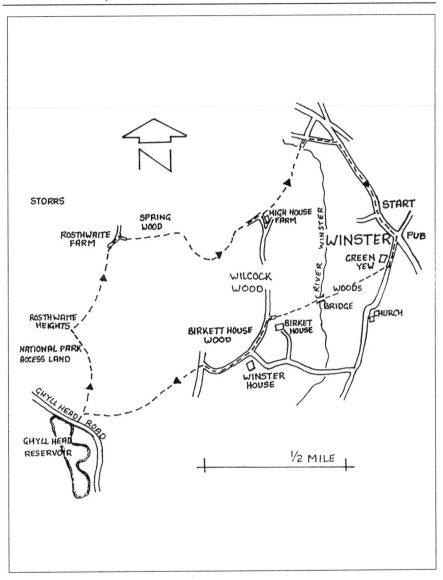

"surprise" view, over the wide expanse of the Winster valley, with a backcloth of the Pennine hills in the far distance

Carry on downhill, turn left at a more important track, and continue to descend the valley side. Just after a "private" gate, go straight ahead through a farm gate, bend left then right along the foot of woodland, the track now being less well defined. At the end of the wood is a steep little rise, followed by further descent to the right. Don't go through an inviting gap in a collapsed wall, but continue along a rudimentary path above swamp to a gate and a primitive bridge over a stream.

Turn right to take the obvious stream-side path towards the public road. Just before the road, pass across the front of a house. Turn right at the road to return to the car park.

```
┌─────────────────────────────────────────────────────────┐
│                                                           │
│          5. Windermere and Bowness                        │
│                                                           │
└─────────────────────────────────────────────────────────┘
```

Length: 3 miles

Rise and Fall: 230 feet (70 metres), comprising a long but very gentle rise through Rayrigg Wood and a short but steep ascent at Millbeck Stock.

Underfoot: Very good throughout. Almost half a mile along the side of Rayrigg Road.

Car Parking: When approaching Bowness from Windermere village, Longlands Road is a right turn just below the cinema. There is a fair amount of parking space a little further on the right, towards the rugby ground. Grid reference 405972. Alternatively, use one of the public car parks in Bowness.

Map: Ordnance Survey Outdoor Leisure no. 7, The English Lakes, south eastern area 1:25,000, or Landranger no. 97, Kendal to Morecambe 1:50,000

Description

A gentle ramble, largely on footpaths within what is probably the most visited town/village in the whole of the Lake District, but yet avoiding the busiest tourist areas. Included are Rayrigg Wood and a beautiful length of the Windermere shore.

Windermere and Bowness are so well known that a lengthy description of their many features of interest to visitors would be out of place here. Bowness is the holiday town, often overrun in high season, but with a very old core behind the fine parish church of St. Martin, rebuilt in the 14th century and refurbished in Victorian times. The east window is splendid, with some glass salvaged from Cartmel Priory at the time of the dissolution of the monasteries. As a resort, the bustling boating activity on Bowness Bay is probably the most attractive feature. The author's "Town and Village Trails of Cumbria and the Lake District" (Sigma Press)

Low Millerground , Windermere

includes a suggested route highlighting historic and other aspects of Bowness.

Windermere is an altogether newer settlement, growing rapidly from almost nothing following the arrival of the railway in 1847. The result is an almost totally Victorian town centre, much less obviously dedicated to tourism than its neighbour, well separated from the lake from which it took its name. Happily, the railway is still functional, providing a service much appreciated by both residents and visitors.

A striking feature common to both Windermere and Bowness is the large house or "villa" built by wealthy merchants, often cotton magnates from the Manchester area, in the early to mid 19th. century. Many have since become hotels. One of the great pastimes of the gentry during the latter part of the last century and the early part of the present century was the ownership and use of elegant steam launches on the lake. Many of these fine craft have been preserved and, beautifully restored, can be seen at the Windermere Steamboat Museum on Rayrigg Road.

The construction of St. Mary's church in 1848 was part of the great mid century development of Windermere. The cost of £1000 was met by the first incumbent, Rev. J.A. Addison.

Route

Start along the surfaced private road (Longlands Road) heading for Rayrigg Wood. Go straight ahead at a junction to continue through attractive mixed woodland. This is largely ancient woodland, privately owned, but subject to a management scheme in conjunction with the Lake District Planning Board. The wide trackway loses its surface as it rises steadily but gently.

Leave the wood at a gate and continue along the surfaced Beemire Road. The land to the left was part of a 19th. century golf course. At Birthwaite Road, with its broad verges, turn left for 150 metres, then right at a signposted footpath. Turn left at a broader track (Old College Lane), pass the old cottages at Low Birthwaite and a sheltered housing complex before reaching the main A591 road by the side of St. Mary's church.

Turn left, cross the entrance to St. Mary's Park, then turn left again to take a footpath before the Cedar Manor Hotel. This well used path descends steadily between the gardens of large and not so large houses to reach an iron gate giving access to Rayrigg Road..

Cross the road, bearing slightly left to a wooden gate, entering Miller Ground (National Trust). The path now descends more steeply to the lake shore, accompanied by Winlass Beck, rushing eagerly in rapids and mini waterfalls alongside. Cross a small bridge before the old house at Low Miller Ground. From here an early ferry crossed the widest part of the lake to Belle Grange on the Claiffe shore. The missing bell was used to summon the ferryman.

Turn left along the shore, passing a traditional Windermere boathouse and jetties. Go through a kissing gate on the left, then through a further gate to continue along the delectable path among the trees by the lake shore, with fine picnic spots in

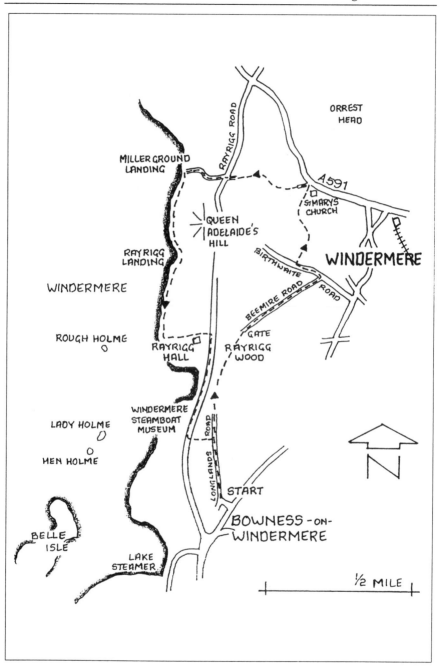

profusion. Fork right to reach the public access area at Rayrigg landings, which has picnic tables and barbecue, with a car park and public conveniences not too far away.

Keep close to the lake until an old iron gate is reached, just before the path comes to an abrupt end. Turn left to leave the lake here, crossing a meadow on a permissive footpath to reach Rayrigg Road. On the right is the historic Rayrigg Hall, for some years the home of the great anti-slavery campaigner, William Wilberforce. Turn right and use the roadside footpath for almost half a mile.

About 50 metres after crossing Mill Beck, by the Steamboat Museum, turn left at a signposted footpath. The track is sharply uphill but, fortunately, only for a short distance. The cottages and fine bank barn comprise Millbeck Stock, a very old outlying hamlet of Bowness. Longlands Road is soon reached. Turn right to return to the car parking area.

---

6. Ambleside and Rydal

Length: 3½ miles

Rise and Fall: Negligible.

Underfoot: Entirely good. The minor road under Loughrigg is sufficiently quiet to be perfectly acceptable to walkers. The main road section is less than half a mile in length, with a roadside footpath.

Car Parking: Main public car park in Ambleside, at Rydal Road. Grid reference 376047.

Map: Ordnance Survey Outdoor Leisure no. 7, English Lakes, south eastern area, 1:25000 or Landranger no. 90, Penrith and Keswick. 1:50,000.

Description

A genuinely level circuit, linking the extremely popular town of Ambleside with Rydal hamlet and Rydal Hall. Although never far from civilisation, there are good mountain views, and the Rydal Hall parkland is quietly attractive.

Despite the pressures of tourism, Ambleside is still a fine little town, with useful shops and plenty of inns and other refreshment opportunities.

Rydal is famed for its William Wordsworth connections. The poet lived at Rydal Mount from 1813 until his death in 1850, during which time the owner of the Hall (and the Mount), Lady Diana le Fleming, paid for the construction of Rydal church, which has since been enlarged. Inside the church are the pews used by Wordsworth and by Dr. Arnold. Behind the church is Dora's field, purchased by Wordsworth for the construction of a house when he believed that his tenancy of the Mount was likely to be terminated. The field is named after his daughter, but the

Bridge House, Ambleside

splendid daffodils are not those which are immortalised in his best known poem.

Rydal Mount is open to visitors during most of the year. Rydal Hall is used as a retreat centre for the Diocese of Carlisle, with a youth centre and camping arrangements for large numbers of young people.

More of the fascinating features of both Ambleside and Rydal are revealed in the author's "Town and Village Discovery Trails of Cumbria and the Lake District" (Sigma Press), either or both of which combine well with the present walk.

Route

From the main Ambleside (Rydal Road) car park, turn left along the main road towards Grasmere. There is a roadside footpath for the comparatively short distance of this unavoidable road walk. Opposite the car park exit is the pleasant complex of Charlotte Mason college, in recent years an outpost of Lancaster University. The old building was formerly the home of the celebrated Harriet Martineau.

Just after crossing Scandale Beck, cross the road to an obvious lodge, with iron gates and a footpath sign "Rydal Hall". Follow the broad track rising very gently through attractive parkland for approximately one mile to the hall. Ahead is the ridge of Heron Pike and Great Rigg, leading the eye towards Fairfield, at the crest of the well known horseshoe walk. Across the valley is the bulk of Loughrigg, with Crinkle Crags and Bowfell peeping through the gap above Red Bank. As the hall is approached, the track passes through light and well varied woodland, with some good specimen trees.

At a junction close to the hall, the well signposted path turns right, uphill. However, a small (permissive) diversion through a gate allows access to a bridge over Rydal Beck with a fine view of the lower Rydal waterfall. This view was admired by, among many others, both Constable and Turner. Immediately below is an inconspicuous building, now a chapel which is kept locked.

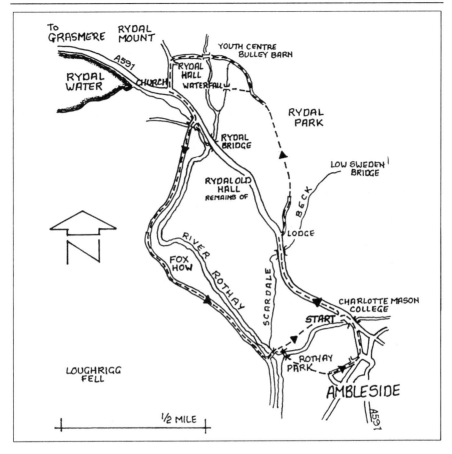

Dating from 1669, this was one of the first "viewing houses" in the country, with its only window facing the fall to provide a framed "picture" of great charm. Ahead are two large blocks of stone being worked from time to time by the famous local sculptress Josefina de Vasconcellos and her students.

Return to the path, which pass through the outbuildings of the hall, including the Bulley Barn and a youth centre. Close to the latter building is sited a turbine which provides the electricity for all the buildings on the site. For a peep at a fine figure of Christ sculpted by Josefina, go through a gate in the wall on the left and turn right. Return to the path to pass around the rear of the hall, its oldest part, and pass the tea shop to reach the road a little way below Rydal Mount.

Turn left to descend to the main road, passing Rydal church. Turn left to follow the main road for a short distance, then turn right over a bridge to take a minor road crossing the water meadows. Accompanied by the River Rothay, this quiet road provides a good walking route, undulating pleasantly around the foot of Loughrigg, with views of Wansfell, over Ambleside town, and of the ridge which leads over Snarker Pike and Red Screes.

One notable house along the way is Fox How, built by Dr. Arnold, the well known headmaster of Rugby school, with a good deal of advice from his friend and neighbour, William Wordsworth of Rydal Mount.

After about 1¼ miles, turn left over an elegant and substantial (packhorse?) bridge across the river. Either go straight ahead to return directly to the car park or fork right to cross Stockghyll Beck and Rothay Park and reach Ambleside by the parish church.

7. Vale of Grasmere

Length: 3 miles

Rise and Fall: 200 feet (61 metres) in total, mainly by Allan Bank. No steep gradients.

Underfoot: Two short rough stony sections, otherwise an excellent mixture of lanes and footpaths. The minor road passing Under Helm Farm is very quiet. The main road (less than half a mile) is usually busy, but there are wide verges and a tarmac footpath on one side.

Car Parking: Small pay and display car park on Easedale Road, a quarter of a mile from Grasmere village centre. Grid reference 334079. In high season this car park may be full. A suggested alternative is the long lay-by beside the main A591 road a quarter of a mile north of the Swan Hotel. Grid reference 338085.

Map: Ordnance Survey Outdoor Leisure no. 7, English Lakes, south eastern area, 1:25,000 or Landranger no. 90, Penrith and Keswick, 1:50,000.

Description

This walk is a basically gentle circular tour of that part of the Vale of Grasmere situated between the village and the sharply rising Helm Crag. With its enduring popularity, Grasmere needs little introduction or description. For a guided walk around its many charming and interesting features, which can advantageously be combined with the present walk, the author's "Town and Village Discovery Trails of Cumbria and the Lake District" (Sigma Press) will provide the perfect companion.

Suffice it to say here that the range of shops and refreshment opportunities is considerable and that the church is much more attractive inside than out. The graves of several of the Wordsworth family, including William himself, are easily found towards the back wall of the churchyard.

Grasmere, The Green

Allan Bank, built in 1805, which features in this walk, is a fair sized house on a knoll, overlooking village and lake. Its construction in such a prominent position and the white painting of the walls annoyed Wordsworth at the time of his occupation of Dove Cottage, from which area Allan Bank struck a discordant note in the otherwise harmonious landscape. Oddly enough, two years later, with a fast growing family, the great poet moved to Allan Bank, living there until the owner wished to occupy the house himself in 1811. He did try to soften the landscape impact by planting a fair number of trees below the house.

Route

From the car park walk back along Easedale Road towards Grasmere village. In less than 150 metres turn right through an old iron gate, with a signpost "Score Crag and Langdale". Bear right over the grass behind two substantial properties. Dominant ahead is the well proportioned house, Allan Bank.

At a junction of paths bear left. There is a "footpath to Langdale"

National Trust sign. The way is uphill but not very steep or prolonged. On reaching a surfaced driveway, turn sharp right, continuing to rise steadily. The fine views certainly make the effort very worthwhile. Ahead is a classic view of Helm Crag, looking every inch a real mountain despite its modest height, whilst across the vale Seat Sandal, surely one of Lakeland's least climbed mountains, stands alone, separated from the Fairfield group by the deep cleft of the Grisedale pass. Stone Arthur juts forward towards Grasmere, with the long ridge which leads over Heron Pike and Great Rigg to Fairfield behind.

At a small old farmstead, the ways divide. Keep right towards Goody Bridge, and then leave the lane to turn right at a gate with yellow arrow. The route is now downhill, over grass, forking right in 20 metres, where the path appears to divide. The descent is quite steep in part, aiming for a ladder stile by the Easedale Beck Go over and cross the beck on stepping stones, large and flat topped. The beckside area is attractive, with small rapids upstream. Follow a yellow arrow to a little gate and pass by Goody Bridge Farm to reach the Easedale Road.

Turn left, and in less than 300 metres turn left again to cross a footbridge over the beck, signposted to Easedale Tarn. The stony path is so popular that major repairs have been carried out to the first section. The well known waterfalls can be seen clearly ahead. In approximately 300 metres turn right to cross a railway sleeper farm bridge over the beck and take a well marked track across the valley leading to the hamlet at the foot of the approved route up Helm Crag.

Turn right along the surfaced roadway, turning left in less than 300 metres to go through an iron gate by the side of a house named Helm End. An unsurfaced lane rises a little, crossing the drive leading to Lancrigg, and passing a youth hostel, before reaching a minor road, with the long, low building of the Traveller's Rest Inn in view half a mile away, across the vale.

Turn left to follow the road, passing the old working farm of Under Helm, and descending to a fine little Lakeland bridge close to the confluence of the River Rothay and a tributary beck. At the

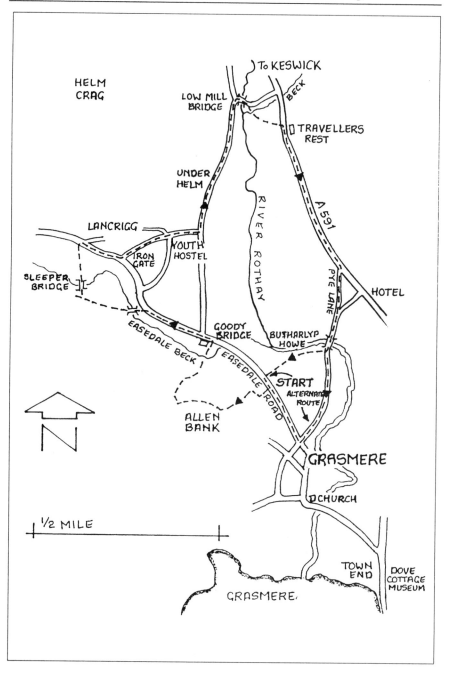

road junction turn right, then turn right again in 30 metres at an old kissing gate with a public footpath signpost. The beck is crossed on stepping stones, posing no problem for the reasonably nimble! Go through a second, way marked, kissing gate and keep close to the wall along the edge of a meadow, always aiming generally towards the Traveller's Rest Inn.

Reach the main road and turn right towards the village. In less than half a mile fork right into Pye Lane. Pass Slapsones Gallery and the White Bridge Forge before crossing the road bridge over the River Rothay. Immediately after the bridge turn right at a gate with a National Trust sign "Butterlip Howe" (the Ordnance Survey uses the spelling "Butharlyp")

A diversion into the village for a wide range of shops, refreshments, and public conveniences is made by continuing along the roadside, with a return to the car park along Easedale Road.

A wide, inviting, track soon becomes a little narrower and rougher underfoot as it rises beside the river through thin woodland with mature silver birches and plenty of young oaks. Easedale Road is soon reached. Turn right to return to the car park.

8. Great Langdale and Mickleden

Length: 2½ miles

Rise and Fall: 100 feet (30 metres) approximately, most of which occurs at the beginning of the walk. No steep gradients.

Underfoot: Rough and stony track along Mickleden. Return by surfaced farm access road.

Car Parking: National Trust pay and display car park at the Old Dungeon Ghyll Hotel. Grid reference 286061.

Map: Ordnance Survey Outdoor Leisure no. 6, The English Lakes, south western area 1:25000, or Landranger no. 90, Penrith and Keswick, 1:50,000.

Description

This undemanding circuit provides a fine opportunity to ramble easily but yet close to the heart of some of Lakeland's most dramatic mountain scenery, with the great peaks of Bowfell, the Crinkle Crags, and Langdale Pikes close at hand. The walk is based on the historic Old Dungeon Ghyll Hotel, formerly combined with a farm, now having a wide range of catering available.

Quite apart from the scenery, the head of Great Langdale is of great landscape and historic interest. Firstly, it is a perfect example of a valley shaped by glacial action, with the scraped sides laying bare the hard rock of the Borrowdale Volcanic series and reminding us that the final retreat of the glaciers in this area was a mere 10,000 years ago. Secondly, with the original tree cover of the valley having gone by about 1000 B.C. as a result of prehistoric farming activity, a well defined pattern of land use at least from medieval times is evident. Those with an eye for historic landscape will notice that at some time in the past at least part of the valley bottom land has been ploughed. Crops such as oats were not uncommon in Lakeland, particularly when contin-

Middle Fell Farm, near Old Dungeon Ghyll

gencies such as the Napoleonic Wars brought a great deal of marginal land under the plough.

Not very many centuries ago this limited amount of land was shared between no less than six farmsteads, four of them close together at what is now Stool End Farm. No wonder the intake walls were pushed high up the valley sides as the farmers wrested just a little more "improved" land from the mountains.

Route

Start along the track rising behind the hotel and follow the wide, unmistakable path which soon levels out by the side of a stone wall. This is one of the great walkers' routes to the fells, trodden by generations of those en route to Scafell or to Borrowdale via the Langstrath valley. It is rough and stony underfoot but otherwise entirely straightforward.

The height gained initially proves to have been well worth the modest effort, the "gallery" effect enhancing the magnificent

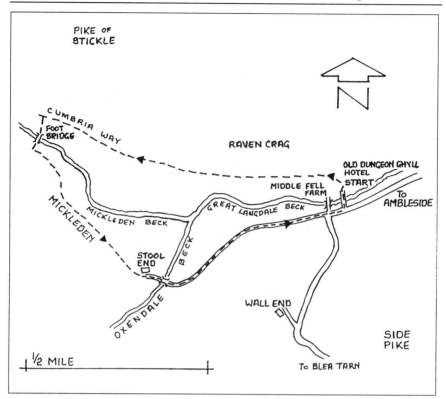

views. Pike o' Blisco is away to the left, then Crinkle Crags, with Bowfell ahead. Even though the valley widens at the junction of Mickleden and Oxendale, it is hard to imagine sufficient productivity to support six farms and the families involved. With care, the site of one of the long demolished farmsteads can be spotted. There are also clearance pile of stones in some fields bearing witness to the efforts made by early farmers to improve the quality of this precious land.

As the track bends a little to the right, the fine cone of Pike o' Stickle comes into view. On its near side is the great scree shoot which has the site of the prehistoric "stone axe factory". Using stones from a band of particularly hard rock, Neolithic men shaped axe heads here which were used both locally and further afield throughout Britain.

At the end of the wall on the left, turn left. The head wall here provides a sharp definition between the farmed land and the rough grazing. To the right are the remains of the structures of a very early settlement, probably from the time when the Norse settlers ("Vikings") were pushing their summer grazing high into the Lakeland valleys.

Cross the river by the footbridge, with a weir and pond to the right. Turn left, soon bending away from the river to join a broader track. The path bends right (footpath sign) then left below a comparatively recent National Trust plantation. Go through a sprung gate and continue to the farm, joining another of the great fell routes as it descends from Bow Fell via the Band.

Go through a gate with a "path" sign, traverse the buildings of this National Trust farm, and leave by the farm access road. Cross Oxendale Beck, its flooding tendencies tamed by the very unsightly canal-like protection works, and continue along the surfaced farm road all the way to the public road. The small mountain ahead is Side Pike, the north western end of the Lingmoor ridge.

At the public road go ahead for 50 metres and turn left to the Old Dungeon Ghyll and its car park. Before this turning, however, look along the access roadway to Middle Fell farm, where there is an old packhorse bridge.

---

9. Elterwater and Little Langdale

Length: 3 miles (shorter version 2¼ miles)

Rise and Fall: 530 feet (162 metres) approx. Two thirds of this total occurs as a continuous ascent on the lane from Elterwater.

Underfoot: Excellent lane and good, if occasionally indistinct, footpaths. Minimal length of minor road.

Car Parking: Restricted parking in Elterwater generally. National Trust car park opposite the Britannia Inn. Grid reference 329047; or, free car park at foot of common on other side of main road. Grid reference 329051.

Map: Ordnance Survey Outdoor Leisure no. 7, The English Lakes, south eastern area, 1:25000 or Landranger no. 90, Penrith and Keswick, 1:50,000.

Description

Although quite short, this walk is fairly demanding in terms of ascent. The lane through the woods from Elterwater rises more than 300 feet (91 metres) in a comparatively short distance. Fortunately, the going underfoot is first rate. The return route crosses the same ridge of high ground at a lower point and the ascent is correspondingly less.

Elterwater, in Great Langdale, renowned as a lovely Lakeland village, is provided with post office/stores, public conveniences and the Britannia Inn. The nearby common must be one of the finest picnic areas in the whole of the country. This walk combines Elterwater with the less populated but undoubtedly beautiful Little Langdale valley. There is no village in this valley, but the Three Shires Inn is available for en route refreshment.

Route

From the centre of Elterwater village, by the Britannia Inn, follow the road to the south, crossing Great Langdale Beck and passing the youth hostel. In less than a quarter of a mile turn right, opposite the Eltermere Hotel. The road goes steadily uphill. Leave the tarmac road at a "footpath Little Langdale" signpost and continue to rise rather steeply on an excellent stony lane, through fine woodland.

Towards the top of the rise views open up the left and most of the Little Langdale valley is soon in view. Ahead is Wetherlam, with Swirl How and Great Carrs, also of the Coniston group of fells, to its right.

A kissing gate on the left is the start of the shorter version of the walk. For this route, another left fork in a short distance leads across farmland to rejoin the full route close to Low Hackett

The main route continues along the lane to Dale Head Farm, becoming surfaced from the farm to its junction with the valley road. Turn left along the roadside to descend past the chapel to

Little Langdale

the Three Shires Inn. A short distance after the Inn, turn left at Wilson Place Farm where there is a signposted track to Elterwater. Be careful here to ignore the well used route ahead and to turn right opposite the farmhouse, to a gate with a yellow arrow on a post behind.

Follow a track worn by farm vehicles to a gate with a "footpath" board and arrow. The track hereabouts is not very obvious; stay

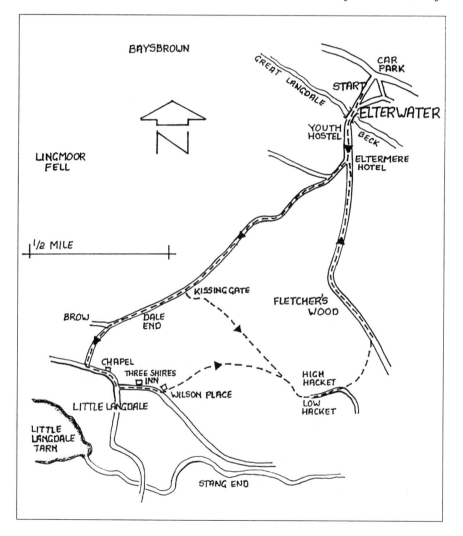

parallel with the wall on the right. Views behind include the Little Langdale valley head, Crinkle Crags and the summit of Lingmoor. Go over a stile with arrow at the top of the meadow, then up a few steps to a gate. A large meadow is now crossed , with the path barely obvious. Aim for the lower fringe of the trees to the left, then for the gateway in the wall ahead.

Angle slightly right to a gate/stile with arrow, then over two more walls in quick succession, with a turn to the left included. Here the path is twisting its way around the grounds of Low Hackett, a substantial house. An "Elterwater" sign points the way to a stile over another wall and the Low Hackett approach driveway. Follow the drive downhill to a long right bend, then turn left at an "Elterwater" finger post.

An obvious path carries on downhill to a stile giving entry to Fletcher's Wood (National Trust). The path is very clear as it descends through the wood to join the Elterwater to Colwith road. Turn left to return to Elterwater village. Elterwater itself is visible over the wall to the right of the road.

10. Far Sawrey and Moss Eccles Tarn

Length: Full circuit 5¼ miles. Moss Eccles Tarn and Near Sawrey 3 miles.

Rise and Fall: Full circuit – so many rises and falls that it is difficult to calculate – probably between 700 and 800 feet (213 – 244 metres). Short walk – approximately 270 feet (74 metres).

Underfoot: The outward half is on broad easy tracks but the return includes a fair amount of rougher footpath, with tree roots and stony surface. Short walk – entirely easy.

Car Parking: Small car park at Village Institute, Far Sawrey, almost opposite the Sawrey Hotel. Box for contributions to Institute funds. Probably not available when there is a function at the Institute. Grid reference 379954.

Map: Ordnance Survey Outdoor Leisure no. 7, The English Lakes, south eastern area, 1:25,000 or Landranger no. 97, Kendal to Morecambe, 1:50,000.

Description

Moss Eccles Tarn is a most attractively situated small lake easily reached from either Near or Far Sawrey. The shorter walk described here, from Far Sawrey to the tarn, returning via Near Sawrey, is particularly appropriate for a fine day, with a tarnside picnic.

The longer walk comes with a definite "health" warning for level walkers. Although not very long, in its traverse of Claiffe Heights it has the greatest amount of rise and fall of any basic walk in the book. The very name Claiffe Heights does sound a cautionary note: additionally, perhaps 25% of the route is rough underfoot. The reward for those who opt for this circuit is a well

Near Moss Eccles Tarn

varied walk through an interesting area with some great view-points en route.

Near and Far Sawrey are attractive small villages along the road from Hawkshead to the Windermere ferry. The former has Hill Top, Beatrix Potter's former home, long owned by the National Trust and open to visitors from Easter to October. There is also the Tower Bank Arms, a rare example of an inn owned by the National Trust. At Far Sawrey are the Sawrey Hotel and a village shop.

Route

Walk down the road past the Sawrey Hotel, forking right in 100 metres to follow "public bridleway to Moss Eccles Tarn and Claiffe Heights". The surfaced roadway rises, passing the Old Vicarage, with views to the left over Near Sawrey village to the Coniston group of fells.

Go through a kissing gate to head for Righting, an impressive house ahead. Fork left to leave the drive at a "Hawkshead" sign.

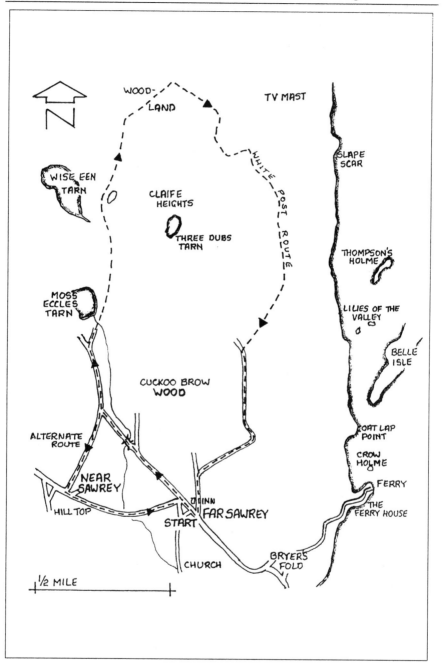

The good broad track crosses Wilfin Beck on a footbridge, rising again to join the similar track from Near Sawrey. Go straight on past a "bridleway, Claiffe Heights" sign, rising again. After a gate there is an area of great rocky slabs before Moss Eccles Tarn is reached. This was a favourite place for Beatrix Potter who for many years kept a rowing boat on the tarn.

For the shorter walk turn round and return to the fork where the broad track to the right descends to Near Sawrey, for Hill Top and the Tower Bank Arms. From Near Sawrey head back along the road, using any roadside paths which may be available, to Far Sawrey and the car park.

To continue to Claiffe Heights stay with the broad track, rising again. Behind, part of Windermere can now be seen. Wise Een Tarn is soon reached and a small reservoir behind a stone faced dam. As height is gained there are views to peaks in the Langdale area. At a crude sign on a rock follow "Hawkshead", soon rising again, now across grass

Enter coniferous woodland at a double gate. There is another small tarn just visible below on the right. Follow a signpost to the right "ferry, Far Sawrey" with a yellow arrow. Underfoot the path is now much more broken up, with stones and tree roots, following numerous wooden posts with white tops. We are following part of the official "White Post Route", soon reaching signpost no. 7. Continue, still uphill, with an old stone wall on the right, reaching the summit of a pine clad hill. This is a superb viewpoint for the Fairfield group of fells and Wansfell Pike, above Ambleside.

Continue downhill, still following the white topped posts, cross a wet hollow on a boardwalk and join a wide, stony roadway at signpost no. 6, turning right "footpath ferry, Far Sawrey". In 100 metres at Signpost no. 5 turn left to follow the same posting, again with white topped posts along the way, downhill and somewhat rough underfoot.

At signpost no. 4 go straight on, again to "ferry, Far Sawrey".

There are glimpses of Windermere and of Bowness village

before the path descends more steeply. Rise to a gate/stile to leave the woodland. To the rear the ridge which includes Yoke, Ill Bell and Froswick can be seen standing impressively above Troutbeck. The broad, stony, track passes a tiny tarn and rises a little before descending to a "T" junction. Turn right to follow "bridleway, Far Sawrey" for the last lap back to the village, reaching the road directly opposite the car park.

11. Hawkshead and Outgate

Length: 3½ miles

Rise and Fall: Less than 200 feet (61 metres) in total. No steep or prolonged ascents.

Underfoot: Good footpaths, unsurfaced lanes and minor road. No difficulty apart from a little mud.

Car Parking: Pay and display car park in Hawkshead village. Grid reference 353981

Map: Ordnance Survey Outdoor Leisure no. 7, The English Lakes, south eastern area, 1:25,000 or Landranger no. 97, Kendal to Morecambe, 1:50,000.

Description

A truly gentle ramble in the delightful countryside around Hawkshead. As probably the most picturesque village in Cumbria, for most visitors Hawkshead will need no introduction. Particular attractions include the Old Grammar School, attended by William Wordsworth, and the National Trust owned gallery where a collection of Beatrix Potter's original water-colours, used to illustrate the famous books, is displayed during the summer season (Easter to October).

The parish church of St. Michael and All Angels is beautifully situated on its knoll above the village. The earliest portions of the building, including the tower, are more than 700 years old. There were large scale extensions and renovations around the year 1300 and again around 1500. Several inns and tea shops provide varied refreshment in the village and there is a good range of other shops.

(For a more thorough appraisal of Hawkshead and a suggested walking route which combines well with the present walk, see

The Old Courthouse

the author's "Town and Village Discovery Trails of Cumbria and the Lake District" – Sigma Press)

The Old Courthouse to the north of the village was the gatehouse, the only surviving part of the former Hawkshead Hall, erected by the monks of Furness Abbey as the administrative centre for their varied activities in this part of their widespread domains. Use of the building as a courthouse was in more recent years. It is now owned by the National Trust. There is little to see inside, but a key is available at the National Trust shop in the middle of Hawkshead.

"Ground" as part of a place name, common around Hawkshead, dates from the dissolution of the monasteries around 1540, in this case Furness Abbey, and the division of their estates, creating new farms. The first part of each name is that of the new landowner at that time.

Route

Cross the village street by the public conveniences and rise past the front of the Old Grammar School towards the church. Go through the gate and across the churchyard, bearing left to leave the churchyard at a small gate. Note the slate on edge field boundaries so typical of this area. Fork right after a kissing gate to follow a public footpath "Tarn Hows, Coniston, Grisedale Forest".

Go through two more gates to continue past the Vicarage and the Old Vicarage to a "T" junction with a rough surfaced lane. Turn left and then right in 25 metres at a kissing gate signposted "Tarn Hows" etc. Go across the meadow to a kissing gate "Keen Ground only" and then straight across another meadow to another waymarked kissing gate. Views to the right include Latterbarrow with its monument and the higher Fairfield group of fells behind Ambleside

Pass to the right of Keen Ground and go through a gate to join the tree lined access roadway. Turn right to descend, with Penrose Beck on the left. Turn left at the Hawkshead to Ambleside road, towards the Old Courthouse, now visible. Turn left at the junction, signposted "Tarn Hows", passing saw mills with a pond at the rear which suggests the use of water power in former days.

Turn right in a further 100 metres or so into a surfaced minor road – Skinners How Lane. In a short distance pass Violet Bank and turn right through a gate with a public footpath sign. Cross a meadow to a kissing gate and a stone slab bridge over a stream. The path rising over grass is reasonably distinct, leading to a stile/gate by a muddy section. Pass the prominent house, Fell field and join a very minor road.

Turn right, downhill, with just a glimpse of Esthwaite Water far to the right. Walk to the Hawkshead to Ambleside road and turn left. A permissive path beside the road leads to Outgate and its inn in less than half a mile

Cross the road and take the footpath beside the inn. There is a signpost on the opposite side of the road. Go through two gates in quick succession to follow an obvious grassy track through more waymarked kissing gates. At the corner of a patch of

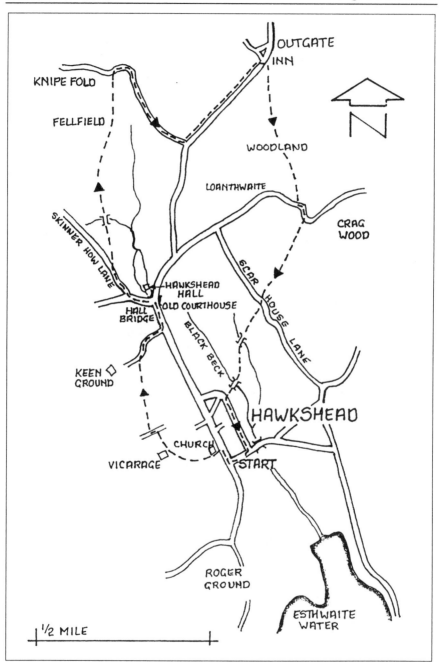

OUTGATE INN

KNIPE FOLD

FELLFIELD

WOODLAND

LOANTHWAITE

SKINNER HOW LANE

CRAG WOOD

HAWKSHEAD HALL

OLD COURTHOUSE

HALL BRIDGE

SCAR HOUSE LANE

KEEN GROUND

BLACK BECK

HAWKSHEAD

CHURCH

VICARAGE

START

ROGER GROUND

ESTHWAITE WATER

½ MILE

woodland go left over a stile and keep to the path as indicated by an arrow on a post in 100 metres.

On emerging from the wood head for a farm gate/stile and on to a farm, bearing right to reach a public road. Turn left along the road for 90 metres, then right at a kissing gate, signposted "public footpath, Hawkshead". The path is well provided with yellow arrows and the village is now set out attractively in front. Go along the edge of a meadow, with fine views of the Coniston group of fells to the right.

Join a narrow, bramble fringed, lane (Scar House Lane). In 50 metres turn right at a gate to take a path signposted to Hawkshead. After another stile and a gate cross a footbridge over a stream, continue towards the village, and turn right to cross Black Beck on a substantial footbridge. A wide track leads up to the road. Turn left to return direct to the car park; go straight across through a waymarked gate for a meander among Hawkshead's attractive buildings.

12. Coniston and Yewdale

Length: 4 miles (a shorter version of 3 miles is available)

Rise and Fall: About 360 feet (110 metres) in total, with a short rise at the start and a steady ascent from Low Yewdale to Back Guard Plantation. No steep gradients.

Underfoot: Good but occasionally stony footpaths, with a little mud. A minimal amount of road within Coniston village and a quarter of a mile on the Coniston to Ambleside road.

Car Parking: Main pay and display car park in Coniston village, well signposted. Modern Tourist Information Centre and public conveniences. Grid reference 303976

Map: Ordnance Survey Outdoor Leisure no. 6, The English Lakes, south western area, 1:25000 or Landranger no. 97, Kendal to Morecambe. 1:50,000.

Description

Another very attractive easy walk based on the popular village of Coniston, visiting two old farmsteads in Yewdale. The route includes woodland and the final elevated section has superb lake and mountain views. Readers of either of the author's "Lakeland Walking on the Level" or "Town and Village Discovery Trails of Cumbria and the Lake District" (both Sigma Press) will be familiar with Coniston's industrial history and its comparatively recent conversion into a centre for tourism, with ample facilities for shopping and refreshment.

Suffice it to say here that the Ruskin grave in the parish churchyard is well worth seeing and that there is a small Ruskin museum at the rear of the village institute, on the main street, closed for refurbishment in 1997. Ruskin's house, Brantwood, is across the lake, open to the public, and accessible by ferry.

Although Coniston is not the prettiest village in Lakeland, the combination of lake, village and mountains provides fine walking opportunities without having to climb those mountains.

Coniston

Route

From the car park turn left towards the village centre, passing the Crown Hotel, tea rooms and assorted shops. The parish church of St. Andrew, mainly Victorian, is by the junction with the main road. Turn right to pass the Black Bull Inn, then left at once into a minor road. Ahead is the impressively steep side of the Yewdale Fells, whilst over the wall to the left Church Beck rushes through the village on its way to the lake. The surfaced road rises steadily as it bends to the right, bordered by rhododendrons and large conifers.

Pass Silver Bank, where the road loses its surface and, at the end of a wall on the right, turn sharp right over an unsignposted stile. An obvious footpath goes along the side of the wall, partly stony, partly grassy, with some mud. Yewdale Fells tower above to the left; to the right, longer views include the television relay mast on Claiffe Heights, above Windermere.

In about a quarter of a mile turn right at a gate to descend a short, stony track to Far End hamlet. Turn left to follow the surfaced road as far as the main road. Turn left towards Ambleside. In 40 metres turn left to leave the road at a gate with a National Trust sign "footpath to Skelwith Bridge avoiding road" The attractive footpath passes easily through woodland, which has plenty of evidence of former coppicing of the timber. As the woodland thins out, Holme Fell shows up well ahead.

Go over two ladder stiles as the path approaches the road.

(A gate on the right may be used to cross the road and follow the bridleway/access road to Low Yewdale for the shorter walk)

Continue along the path and rejoin the road at a gate, carrying on towards Ambleside. Pass two road junctions to reach High Yewdale, an old Lakeland farmstead with a hotch potch of buildings of many generations, including an obvious former cottage in the foreground.

Turn right to leave the road at a "public footpath – Coniston" sign opposite the farm. A level track keeps to the field edge, with a slate on edge boundary, so common around Hawkshead. Bend

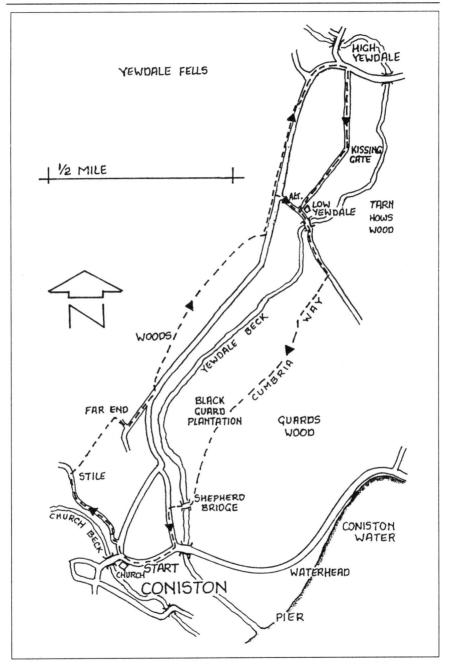

YEWDALE FELLS

HIGH YEWDALE

KISSING GATE

½ MILE

ALT.

LOW YEWDALE

TARN HOWS WOOD

WOODS

YEWDALE BECK

CUMBRIA WAY

FAR END

BLACK GUARD PLANTATION

GUARDS WOOD

STILE

CHURCH BECK

SHEPHERD BRIDGE

CONISTON WATER

CHURCH

START

CONISTON

WATERHEAD

PIER

right at a kissing gate and go across the next field. To the left, Tarn Hows Wood covers the slope. Low Yewdale is approached by a railway sleeper bridge and kissing gate. The strident call of a male peacock might welcome you as you pass straight through the farm, reaching an unsurfaced lane with a signpost.

Turn left for "Boon Crag and Tarn Hows". Cross Yewdale Beck on the bridge and follow the lane as it bends right, rising. In less than a quarter of a mile turn right at a stile/gate to take a just visible path rising invitingly over the grass ahead. As the path becomes a little indistinct, keep straight on to a gate in the wall ahead. Just beyond is a post with yellow sign, under an oak tree. The path soon forks, at another post with yellow arrow. Bear left towards a wall and woodland, still rising.

Enter the wood (Back Guard Plantation) at a gate/stile. In the wood, dark with beech, a few foxgloves lighten the gloom. Leave the wood at a kissing gate and then a stile, to enjoy fine elevated views of Coniston village, with the lake and Coniston Old Man soon coming into sight. The path descends initially among gorse to an unusual ruin, with one surviving wall of a once elegant building. Go left through a kissing gate and continue to another gate and a stile beside the Yewdale Beck

Cross the beck by Shepherd Bridge to reach the public road by the Coniston Primary School. Turn left, then right at a "T" junction to return towards the village centre and the car park.

13. Eskdale

Length: 3¾ miles

Rise and Fall: 50 metres (165 feet) No long or steep ascents

Underfoot: Generally good footpaths and bridleways. Some mud and just a little stony ground. Nearly one mile on the valley road, quiet except perhaps in high season.

Car Parking: Roadside area for six or seven vehicles at foot of Hardknott Pass. Grid reference, 213012. Alternatively, there are larger roadside areas less than a quarter of a mile further down the road.

Map:s Ordnance Survey Outdoor Leisure no. 6, The English Lakes, south western area, 1:25,000 or Landranger no. 89, West Cumbria, 1:50,000.

Description

An excellent walk with very little rise and fall linking the foot of the well known Hardknott Pass with the ancient farmstead of Brotherikeld, the Woolpack Inn, and Doctor Bridge. The scenery in this part of mid Eskdale is very fine; Scafell, Scafell Pikes, Esk Pike and Bowfell are all in view, not far away, whilst Harter Fell dominates the south side of the valley, close at hand.

Doctor Bridge is a wide spanned old packhorse bridge, widened in 1734 by the then resident of Penny Hill nearby so that he could cross with his pony and trap. As no attempt was made to match the curve of the existing arch, the widening is very obvious. The bridge was on the shortest route for the packhorse traders carrying wool between Whitehaven and Kendal; the nearby Woolpack Inn was a favoured stopping place.

Close to the line of the walk with its terminus at Dalegarth is the Ravenglass and Eskdale Railway, a wonderful visitor attraction with fine steam hauled trains throughout the season and a

Eskdale

very restricted diesel service in winter (ref. the author's "Lakeland Walking on the Level" – Sigma Press – for a walk incorporating a ride on the railway). At nearby Boot is a restored water powered corn mill, open to visitors.

A little further away, high beside the road over the Hardknott Pass, is the wonderfully sited and well restored Roman fort of the same name, with its bird's eye view down the valley.

Route

Walk down the road and turn right by the telephone box into a broad unsurfaced track giving access to Brotherikeld Farm (National Trust). As the farm is reached bear left to follow a small, rather temporary looking, sign. Cross a small stream on a sleeper bridge an then go through a kissing gate signposted "Esk Falls and Bowfell. Over bridge to Taw House and Scafell". The well shaped peak in view at the head of the valley is Bowfell.

Turn left to cross the River Esk on a high footbridge and go over

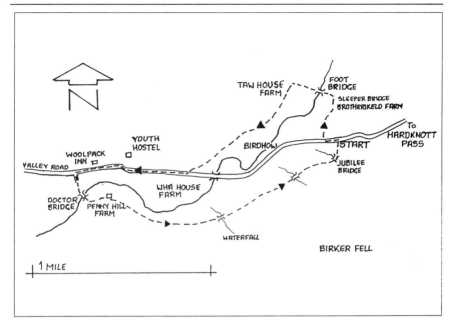

a stile to follow a good track, with further stiles, to Taw House
Farm. Go over a ladder stile into the farm yard. Turn left and keep
left to leave the farm by its broad, unsurfaced, access roadway.
Across the valley, Harter Fell is the dominant peak.

Pass Birdhow and join the valley road, keeping right and soon
passing Wha House Farm, below to the left. Except at really busy
times the road is perfectly acceptable to walkers, passing the fine
and long established youth hostel before reaching the Woolpack
Inn.

In about 200 metres turn left at a surfaced cul de sac road
signposted to Penny Hill Farm. Descend to the river; by Doctor
Bridge is a choice picnic area. Cross the bridge and fork left
towards Penny Hill Farm, at one time an inn. Go straight through
the farm yard then after a blue arrow on a gate post, bend right
into a walled lane.

An easy and generally level track now returns along the valley
side. As this track forks at a waymarked post, keep left. A possibly
muddy area by a gate is passed and there are more waymarks.

After a gate/stile, cross a rushing, tumbling, stream and reach a signpost by a wall. Go straight on to follow "footpath, Hardknott". To the right, uphill, is a path to a small waterfall.

The grassy track now rises a little through bracken before a left fork leads to a plank bridge over Doddknott Gill and then to a gate in the wall ahead. The path is now much narrower but still easy to follow, through sparse woodland. There are occasional stiles along the way and the superb views include Scafell, Scafell Pikes and Bowfell.

Traverse more open hillside, go through a kissing gate, descend a little and then join a wider path which has descended the hillside on the right. Go through two more kissing gates and down a stony track to cross Hardknott Gill by the tiny Jubilee Bridge. Climb the far side to return to the parking area.

14. Ennerdale

Length: 8 miles

Rise and Fall: For more than 95% of the circuit this walk is virtually level with not much more than 50 feet (15 metres ascent) in aggregate. However, one short section at Anglers' Crag climbs steeply up and down two or three times, perhaps 100 feet (30 metres) in total.

Underfoot: Apart from a little mud the outward half is very good indeed largely on wide trackways, some surfaced. The return path is much rougher, largely stony and, in part, artificially improved. At Anglers' Crag there are two very minor scrambles down rocks, safe and not in any way exposed.

Car Parking: Substantial car park by Bleach Green Cottage, accessed from Ennerdale Bridge. After heading east from Ennerdale Bridge take the right fork in half a mile, bear left then right to cross the River Ehen before parking. Grid reference 085153

Map: Ordnance Survey Outdoor Leisure no. 4, The English Lakes, north western area, 1:25,000 or Landranger no. 89, West Cumbria, 1:50,000.

Description

One of the longer walks in the book, this is a more attractive circuit than might be expected by those who have regarded Ennerdale as a valley full of dull coniferous plantations. For reasons of non-accessibility Ennerdale has always been Lakeland's most peaceful and secluded major valley. Its great glory is the view over the lake to a wonderful mountain panorama, all the more interesting for being less familiar than, say, Langdale or Borrowdale. Pride of place goes to Pillar, one of the select group of great fells which exceed 2,900 feet (839 metres) in height but do not quite reach the magical 3,000 feet (914 metres). Great Gable and Bowfell are the others. The huge but-

Ennerdale Water

tress below the summit plateau is Pillar Rock, according to the late A. Wainwright "the most handsome crag in Lakeland".

Apart from the tranquil Ennerdale Water, the other main scenic feature is the commercial planting of huge areas of dull, regimented conifers by the former Forestry Commission from the 1930s, rightly criticised by many writers and others who love Lakeland and deplore spoliation of its fragile landscape. Fortunately, efforts have been made to ameliorate the damage and, apart from some unacceptable straight edges visible on the slopes of Great Borne, the route of this walk is hardly affected.

The other great controversy in Ennerdale has been water abstraction, which for many years has been carried out on a comparatively small scale. An important legal battle was fought in 1978/82, when British Nuclear Fuels (Sellafield) and the North West Water Authority both proposed to take water on a much larger scale from Ennerdale Water and Wastwater. Fortunately, at the Public Inquiry opposition by conservation bodies and by a variety of local people proved to be too strong and the proposals were rejected, a decision of importance for the particular issue and a warning for other bodies which might consider one form or other of commercial exploitation of Lakeland. One has only to look at Thirlmere or Haweswater in a dry summer to realise what damage to this lovely lake would have resulted from a contrary decision.

Route

Leave the car park through a high kissing gate and take a gravelled path close to the river. Join a roadway and continue to the lake. Turn left to cross the River Ehen on a footbridge. The weir and associated works remind us that the lake does provide water on a limited scale for the population of West Cumbria.

Go through a kissing gate and follow a well used path by the shore, passing a Scout camp and a plantation of silver birch trees. Continue through the National Trust "Ennerdale" land, crossing Rothay Sike, a small stream. The route is very easy to follow via gates and stiles but one section is muddy due to cattle access and movement. White painted Beckfoot Farm is in view ahead as a area of gorse is passed.

Turn right after a stile/gate to descend a stony lane to the lake shore, then cross a tributary stream on a little bridge. Above, left, are the bare scree scarred slopes of Great Borne, with the lower knoll of Bowness Knott ahead and Crag Fell across the lake. The next landmark ahead is another long low white painted building, Bowness Farm.

Soon, a choice of route is evident; go left up an old lane to reach the Forest Enterprise Bowness Knott car park, with picnic tables, public conveniences (closed in winter) and information board setting out colour coded forest trails, or fork right to stay on a narrow path by the lake shore, avoiding 40 or 50 feet (12 – 15 metres) of ascent. The ways rejoin a little way beyond the car park and continue close to the water as a roadway, part surfaced along the lower edge of Bowness Plantations, commercial forestry but diversified with silver birch and other deciduous trees.

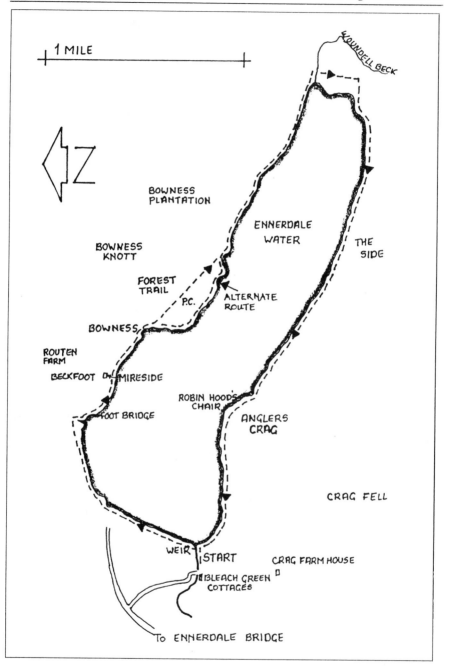

Pillar is now well seen ahead, with Pillar Rock prominent on its northern face. To the right of Pillar, Steeple is visible across the depression of Wind Gap. To the north the valley is bounded by Starling Dodd and then the less spectacular side of the long ridge, including Red Pike (Buttermere), High Stile, High Crag, and Haystacks, which separates Ennerdale from the Buttermere valley.

A tributary stream is crossed by a bridge as the extensive wetland at the head of the lake is approached. A gravel path beside the River Liza (here known as Char Dub) provides an alternative to the roadway. Turn right at a wide junction and cross the river by a low, utilitarian, concrete-topped bridge, with some good picnic spots adjacent. Further up the valley the angular commercial plantations which have given the Forestry Commission such a bad press are very obvious.

Cross the valley bottom and turn right over a ladder stile with a "lakeside path" signpost. A grassy path heads back towards the lake, an inviting greensward among the acres of bracken. Continue along the lake shore, the path always being obvious but becoming more winding and stony and, in part, artificially improved. Enter the National Trust "The Side" at a stile. The path continues in the same style with occasional gates and small bridges.

Close to Anglers' Crag the more exiting part is reached in crossing the side of the crag, which plunges steeply into the lake. There are now several short sharp rises and falls, firstly to cross above a steep scree slope and then over rock, with two downward scrambles, short, not exposed and not in any way dangerous. The path soon resumes its normal benign nature, leading back to the foot of the lake by the weir and on to the car park.

15. Crummock Water

Length: 8 miles

Rise and Fall: Minimum of about 230 feet (70 metres). Use of the two recommended road avoiding sections adds approximately 140 feet (43 metres). No steep gradients.

Underfoot: Apart from a small amount of swampy ground, the paths are very good indeed. A maximum of 2¼ miles is by the side of the valley road, which has generally lightly traffic. The recommended diversions avoid three quarters of a mile of this road.

Car Parking: There are several small free car parks along the valley road, close to the lake. As good as any is one situated 200 metres or so to the north east of Hause Point, half a mile from Buttermere village. Grid reference 163183.

Map: Ordnance Survey Outdoor Leisure no. 4, The English Lakes, north western area. 1:25,000 or Landranger no. 89, West Cumbria, 1:50,000.

Description

Crummock Water, a fine lake owned by the National Trust, is the middle and largest of the Buttermere, Crummock, Loweswater trio. The lake is set predominantly among open mountain scenery, but with enough woodland at the north end to add variety to this excellent walk which circumnavigates the lake. The dominant mountain is the huge bulk of Grasmoor, from the northern end of the lake appearing to be deceptively sharp peaked.

To the south east Crummock shares the wonderful array of mountains at the valley head with its close neighbour Buttermere. Indeed, it is only in comparatively recent times, geologically speaking, that the two lakes have become separated by the accumulation of deposited silt.

Buttermere village is an attractive focal point for visitors to the valley and is provided with The Fish Hotel, Bridge Hotel, Croft

Crummock Water

House Cafe, and public conveniences in the car park behind the Fish. This latter hotel is best known for the true story of the Mary Robinson, "Maid of Buttermere", victim of an infamous bigamist and swindler. Mary obviously recovered well from her unfortunate youthful experience, later living for many years as a farmer's wife in Caldbeck, where she is buried (ref. the author's "Town and Village Discovery Trails of Cumbria and the Lake District" – Sigma Press). Perhaps as a simple country girl she enjoyed the short term relationship with this experienced man of the world and the later, probably short lived, fame arising from the public interest after he had been exposed.

The tiny 19th. century church perches attractively on a knoll above the village.

Route

Set off along the roadside, away from Buttermere, passing Rannerdale Farm. There is walkable grass verge for most of the way. Cinderdale Common, with more car parking areas, is soon reached. The mountains on the right are Whiteless Pike , Crag Hill and Grasmoor. Across the lake is the lower, elongated, Melbreak. Turn left at a kissing gate 120 metres beyond the second of the Cinderdale Common parking areas to enter the National Trust "Fletcher Fields"

Turn right; at first there is some choice of footpath along the gorse clad slope, but all routes lead eventually to a well defined path by the lake shore, with delectable waterside picnic spots. A small shingle beach is crossed before a stile leads into a strip of lakeside woodland, dominated by oaks. The path has been discreetly improved here and there, with little bridges provided across the occasional stream. A gate leads into a plantation of privately owned woodland, with young conifers paramount although there are a few oaks and rowans.

The path continues over stiles into High Wood. The gentle lapping of the water on the lake shore provides a soothing accompaniment for the quiet walker. Pass a boat house. The track becomes wider as it traverses part of Lanthwaite Wood. Fork left at a junction to descend towards the lake. Bear left to go over two footbridges crossing the lake outfall, where the waterworks structures, including a double fish ladder, are reasonably discreet.

Bear left again to keep close to the lake shore. Cross Park Beck on another footbridge and pass the octagonal pump house which has a marble "Workington Corporation" plaque of 1903. Go over the stile to the right and turn left to continue along the shore There is another stile and then a lightly worn grassy path rising a little before descending to a little bay with shingle beach. Go over a ladder stile and keep close to the shore.

The mountains to the east of Crummock Water are now impressively arrayed. From the left are Whiteside, Grasmoor – at first surprisingly sharp – Crag Hill and Whiteless Pike. Lower, but right by the far shore of the lake is Rannerdale Knotts. For the most part the path is well defined, keeping quite close to the shore of the lake, with a little rise and fall and one or two minor swampy areas. As progress is made Grasmoor assumes its more characteristic bulky appearance. Beyond the head of the lake the fine

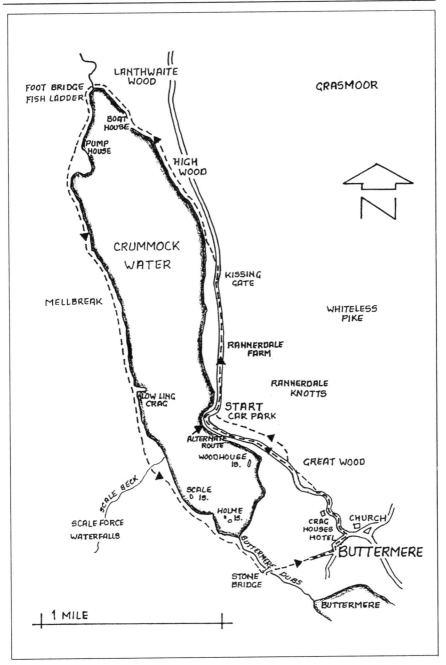

GRASMOOR

LANTHWAITE WOOD

FOOT BRIDGE
FISH LADDER

BOAT HOUSE

PUMP HOUSE

HIGH WOOD

CRUMMOCK WATER

KISSING GATE

MELLBREAK

WHITELESS PIKE

RANNERDALE FARM

RANNERDALE KNOTTS

LOW LING CRAG

START
CAR PARK

ALTERNATE ROUTE

WOODHOUSE 18. 0

GREAT WOOD

SCALE BECK

SCALE 0 15.

HOLME 0 15.

SCALE FORCE
WATERFALLS

CRAG HOUSES HOTEL

CHURCH

BUTTERMERE

BUTTERMERE DUBS

STONE BRIDGE

BUTTERMERE

1 MILE

cluster of mountains is topped by Great Gable's shapely dome. To the right of Great Gable the high ridge above Buttermere includes Red Pike, High Stile, High Crag and Haystacks, beloved of the late A. Wainwright. To the left of Great Gable is Fleetwith Pike, with Honister Crag sitting steeply over the Honister Pass. The pocket handkerchief sized bright green fields at Rannerdale Farm, opposite, stand out in total contrast to the sombre colouring of the mountains all around.

Scales Beck is crossed by a bridge. Up to the right but out of sight is the famous waterfall of the same name, allegedly the highest in Lakeland. A diversion to visit the fall can readily be made; the distance is just over half a mile and the ascent is 300 feet (91 metres). Scale Island is a pretty sight, particularly when Autumn is colouring its tiny array of trees. Continue past the head of the lake; after being joined by the major path to and from Scales Force, the track is wide and well used. At a junction, turn left to cross Buttermere Dubs on a stone bridge and follow the obvious route to Buttermere village.

Turn left in Buttermere to take the valley road, initially uphill. Pass Crag Houses and, in less than a quarter of a mile, fork right into an unmade roadway, rising and falling before rejoining the road.

(If you have had enough of rise and fall, continue along the road)

In 300 metres, by a small informal parking place, fork right along a grassy path rising steadily between the bracken across the lower slopes of Rannerdale Knotts. The total ascent here is about 100 feet (30 metres) and there is a steep little descent on the far side, directly to the car park. The views are great and the path is a joy to walk.

(However, this ascent can be avoided by keeping to the road as it rounds Hause Point)

---

16. Mirehouse and Bassenthwaite Lake

Length: 3¼ miles

Rise and Fall: Almost 350 feet (107 metres), almost all in one prolonged ascent at the start of the walk. The gradient is never really steep and the track is first class.

Underfoot: Very good throughout. Forest trails and field paths with just a little mud here and there. Two hundred metres by the side of the Keswick to Bothel road.

Car Parking: Fair sized Forest Enterprise free car park among the trees at Dodd Wood on the Keswick – Bothel – Carlisle road (A591), across the road from the entrance to Mirehouse. Grid reference 235281. Public conveniences, plenty of picnic tables and the Old Sawmill tea shop.

Map: Ordnance Survey Outdoor Leisure no. 4, The English Lakes, north western area, 1:25,000 or Landranger no. 89, West Cumbria, 1:50,000.

Description

Bassenthwaite is the only true "lake" in the Lake District and this fine circuit gives ample opportunity to admire this splendid sheet of water from vantage points along the lower slopes of Ullock Pike, below Skiddaw. Of enormous interest is the church dedicated to St. Bega, standing lonely close to the lake shore, far from any public road. There are legends concerning the ministry of St. Bega, daughter of an Irish chieftain, from a 7th. century abbey on this site. Many will no doubt have read Melvyn Bragg's "Credo" which builds convincingly on these legends. The present church is certainly of very early origin, probably 10th. century, but was extensively restored in 1874. Inside the church there is much to be seen. The chancel arch is pre-Norman, the transept arch is Norman and the south aisle arch is Early English. The octagonal font is from about 1300 and the wrought iron hour glass holder by the pulpit is of about 1600. The length of sermons was timed, in full view of the congregation, by an hour glass placed in this holder. The Royal Coat of Arms is of King George II, from 1745, the year of Bonnie Prince Charlie, when the congregation perhaps needed to be reminded where their loyalty should lie.

Built originally in 1666 and extended in 1790, Mirehouse has the appearance of a late Georgian manor house. For many years

St Bega's Church

the home of the Spedding family (John Spedding was a school friend of William Wordsworth at Hawkshead), the house was visited on more than one occasion by Tennyson and also by Thomas Carlyle, both friends of the Speddings. Tennyson worked on his "Morte d' Arthur" here and it is widely believed that St. Bega's church close by the lake provided both inspiration and a setting for his famous poem. The house is open to the public, usually on the afternoons of Wednesday, Sunday and Bank Holiday Mondays, from April to October. The gardens are open daily from April to October.

Route

Walk past the public conveniences to the Old Sawmill tea room. Bear right to the footbridge over Skill Beck, noting the broken dam above which created a pool to provide headwater for the wheel which powered the saws in the mill. Turn sharp left after the bridge, towards the road (blue and yellow waymarks) for a short distance, then go uphill to join a surfaced roadway.

Turn right then, in 10 metres turn left and go along a good forest track rising steadily (blue waymark), with Ullock Pike above. There are plenty of young conifers, reminding us that the forest here is a commercial enterprise. Glimpses of the lake are soon obtained. Join another track by a rock face and bear left, now level but soon rising again. The path narrows and begins to descend before crossing Sandbeds Gill.

Continue downhill, now on a broad track. Keep left at a fork. As the road is approached keep right at a fork, heading for the Ravenstone Hotel, and go straight on as the vehicular track bends sharply to the left. Two stiles close to the road now seem to be redundant.

Join the road and turn right, passing the Ravenstone Hotel and Ravenstone Lodge. Turn left immediately after the Lodge. There is a public footpath signpost tucked away in the hedge and there are three steps down from the road. After a gate/stile and some huge conifers, cross a meadow on a lightly used path to a kissing

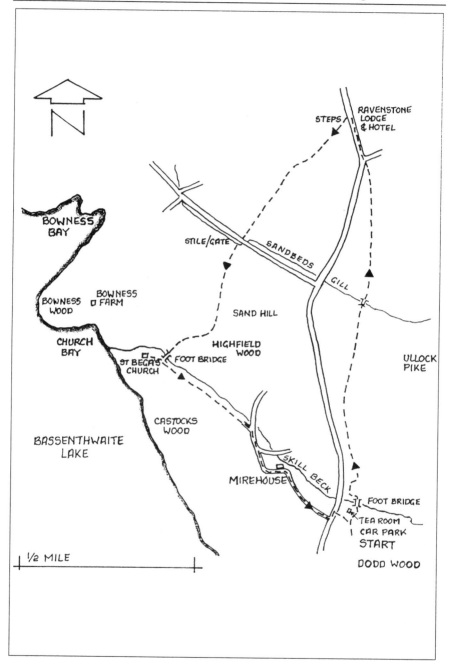

N

BOWNESS
BAY

STEPS

RAVENSTONE
LODGE
& HOTEL

STILE/GATE

SANDBEDS

GILL

BOWNESS
WOOD

BOWNESS
☐ FARM

SAND HILL

CHURCH
BAY

HIGHFIELD
WOOD

ULLOCK
PIKE

ST BEGA'S
CHURCH

FOOT BRIDGE

BASSENTHWAITE
LAKE

CASTOCKS
WOOD

SKILL BECK

MIREHOUSE

FOOT BRIDGE

TEA ROOM

CAR PARK

START

½ MILE

DODD WOOD

gate. Lord's Seat and Broom Fell are the hills straight ahead, on the far side of the lake.

There is a curiously stepped land form in the next field. Walk along the step towards a group of trees and bear left to a tiny stream and a stile over a fence. Continue along the now obvious path among well spaced oak trees. Go through several more kissing gates to a rather incongruous electricity sub station.

Cross a minor road to a gate/stile with a "St. Bega's church" notice. Follow the farm track. Dodd is the conical hill showing well above the wood and the car park of the same name. The farmstead to the left is Sand Hill. A gentle descent along the edge of Highfield Wood leads directly to the church and a modern cross with mounting block marking the site of occasional open air services.

After perusal of the church and its surroundings, retrace footsteps for 50 metres and turn right immediately before the stream to follow a narrow path beside the stream and by a line of great oaks towards Mirehouse. Go through metal gates and keep to the designated footpath through the grounds. Turn right by outbuildings to follow a gravelled driveway, reaching the public road by a gate to the right of a roadside house. Turn left for 40 metres and cross the road to the entrance to the car park and the Sawmill tea room.

17. Stonethwaite, Borrowdale

Length: Basic circuit 2¾ miles, Extendible to 4¾ or 7 miles.

Rise and Fall: Less than 200 feet (61 metres) in total. No steep ascent.

Underfoot: Very mixed. Some rough, stony, path; some wet sections with likely mud, but no significant difficulty.

Car Parking: Area for up to six vehicles in middle of Stonethwaite hamlet, by telephone box. Grid reference 263138. Also a few spaces on wide verges of approach road to hamlet which is situated half a mile off main Borrowdale road, half a mile beyond Rosthwaite.

Map: Ordnance Survey Outdoor Leisure no. 4, The English Lakes, north western area, 1:25,000 or Landranger no. 90, Penrith and Keswick, 1:50,000.

Description

Another very level little walk in the heart of the mountains, although the latter are not so strikingly evident as in the case of, say, the head of Langdale (walk no. 8)

The Langstrath valley is of textbook "U" shape, its regular outline scraped clean by the scouring of the ice only a few thousand years ago. The power and swift run off of the normally abundant rainfall has resulted in persistent flooding of the flat valley bottom around Stonethwaite and Rosthwaite, the floods of 1966 being particularly disastrous.

Several sets of small waterfalls and rapids where the beck has forced its way through weaknesses in the hard "Borrowdale series" granites are most attractive features. Although the upper part of the valley is virtually treeless, the area around and below the junction with Greenup Gill is pleasantly wooded

Stonethwaite ("thwaite" – Norse – "clearing in the forest") is a hamlet with hotel, school and the small church of St. Andrew,

Langstrath, Borrowdale

consecrated in 1687 and subsequently restored and enlarged. The pulpit was brought from the church at Mardale after construction of the reservoir at Haweswater submerged that village.

Route

From the car park by the telephone box start along the "public bridleway, Stake Pass, Langstrath", passing the Langstrath Hotel (which provides bar lunches and other refreshments) to a gate/stile with public footpath sign. A broad easy track follows the valley bottom, with the rocky bulk of Eagle Crag dominating the view ahead. To the right is the long flank of Glaramara.

Go over a ladder stile and through a small area of sparse woodland. A tributary stream, Little Stanger Gill, is crossed, the effects of floodwater on both tributary and the main Stonethwaite Beck being very noticeable. Rise to another ladder stile, the beck hereabouts having fine falls and rapids. After another stile the path becomes more rocky underfoot but is not difficult.

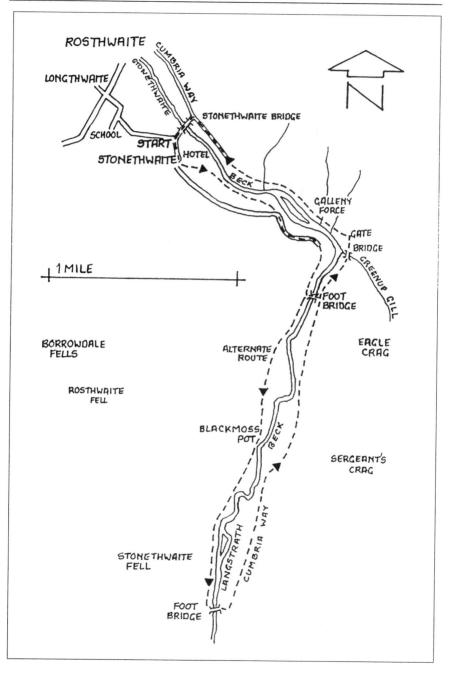

Close to the confluence of Greenup Gill and Langstrath Beck go over a stile in a fence, bear right, and in 40 metres go back over the fence by another stile to join the stony lane which has come directly from Stonethwaite. Continue along the side of Langstrath Beck, with more swift rocky rapids. The track rises but not very much and not steeply. During and after wet weather a good deal of water lies on the surface of the path.

As the more open, desolate, part of the Langstrath valley is reached, with Bowfell visible at the far end, turn left to cross the beck on a footbridge.

For an extended walk visiting the rocky little gorge of Blackmoss Pot continue along the west side of the beck for a further mile and return by the same path unless, during periods of dry weather, you can find a way across the beck. Paddling is, of course, always an option! If so, the return track on the other side will readily be found. Don't be tempted to leap across the narrowest part of the Pot

If you want an even longer walk proceed to the bridge which is another mile or so upstream, then turn left to return.

For the basic circuit cross the bridge, go through a gate and turn left. The path is rocky at first but soon becomes grassy, descending towards the confluence of the two becks. Go through a gate, cross Greenup Gill on a bridge by a grove of small silver birch trees and yet more attractive rapids. Go up to a gate and turn left.

Stonethwaite is in view ahead as the gentle descent commences. Cross a tributary stream, again showing the force of floodwater in this valley and pass Galleny Force where the beck tumbles over rocks in its haste to reach Borrowdale. After a gate the route becomes a narrow lane between walls, one kept in repair and the other neglected. Pass an ash tree and a cluster of very old yews. The way is now entirely straightforward to a signposted junction opposite Stonethwaite hamlet. Turn left here, go through a gate and over a bridge to return to the car park.

18. Castlerigg and St. John's in the Vale church

Length: 4 miles

Rise and Fall: Almost 550 feet (168 metres) in two ascents, the greater being from Naddle bridge to the top of Low Rigg, spread over more than one mile at generally easy gradients. The other rise is from the second crossing of the Naddle Beck up to the main Keswick to Ambleside road, again not steep.

Underfoot: Good, varied walking on footpaths and minor roads (less than one mile). Probably some mud in wet weather.

Car Parking: Roadside lay-by close to the stone circle. Reached by taking the former Penrith road from Keswick (A 5251), turning left at the junction with A 591 towards Penrith, then right in a few yards along a minor road signposted to the Castlerigg stone circle. Grid reference 291237.

Map: Ordnance Survey Outdoor Leisure no. 4, The English Lakes, north western area, 1:25000, or Landranger no. 90, Penrith and Keswick, 1:50000.

Description

Despite the moderate amount of rise and fall, this is a basically easy walk, including one of Lakeland's best known features, the magnificent Castlerigg stone circle. Also visited are the well-situated church of St. John's in the Vale and the little known Tewet Tarn, unremarkable in itself but, like much of this route, rejoicing in being a marvellous viewpoint for most of the mountains of the northern part of the district.

Inevitably, the purpose of the Castlerigg stone circle remains a matter of speculation, although it does have a well defined entrance facing north, and an included small rectangle of stones on the east. The circle is believed to date from the late Neo-

Castlerigg stone circle

lithic/early Bronze ages, 4000 years in round figures. What is certain is that the spectacular setting of this monument is unrivalled.

The church at St. John's in the Vale is Victorian (1845) but is a rebuild of a much earlier church. The solid, low building seems entirely appropriate for its elevated site. One of Lakeland's most celebrated dialect poets, John Richardson (1817-1886), had a long association with the church and the former school, adjacent. He is buried in the churchyard, where there is also a restored sundial.

Route

From the stone circle turn right, down the lane, bending left to Goosewell Farm. The views include mighty Blencathra (Saddleback), firstly on the left and then ahead as the road bends, Great Dodd and Clough Head at the northern end of the Helvellyn range, towering over Low Rigg, our more modest objective, and the valley of the Naddle Beck, close at hand.

Opposite the farm a public footpath sign shows the route of a

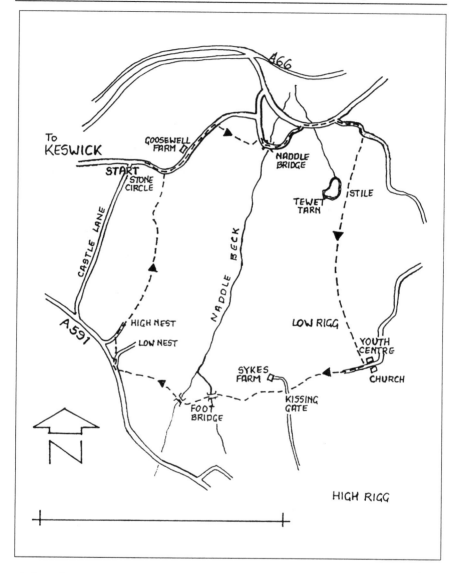

right of way across two fields to Naddle bridge. However, a sign
requests walkers to carry on along the road to a permissive
footpath a little way further . As the extra distance is negligible,
this is a not unreasonable request. A sign and a stile mark the
start of the permissive footpath, which follows the field boundary

for most of the way to the bridge, a little stony but not difficult. Towards the bottom of the field angle left to a ladder stile then rejoin the road at a gate/stile.

Turn right to cross Naddle bridge and follow a very quiet minor road. Turn right at a junction. Turn right again at the next junction, signposted "Shundraw and St. John's in the Vale Diocesan Youth Centre" The road rises gently from Naddle bridge onwards.

Less than a quarter of a mile after the second junction, following right then left bends, turn right at a farm gate with a "public footpath" sign. A wide track angles across a pasture, rising fairly steeply for a "level" walk. Go through a wide gateway at the top. The track soon levels out as it approaches Tewet Tarn. Aim for a stile in the wall about 60 metres to the left of the tarn.

The surroundings of the tarn make an appealing picnic area on a fine day, allowing plenty of time to take in the all round mountain views. In addition to fells already mentioned, Skiddaw rears its elegant shape to the north west, and the north west group of fells, notably Cat Bells, Causey Pike and Grisedale Pike, is well seen from this viewpoint.

The track continues uphill at an easy gradient to a gate/stile, passing close to the highest point of Low Rigg before descending to a stile in the roadside wall and the church and Youth Centre.

Turn right to descend steeply, the road soon losing its surface. At the bottom go through a kissing gate opposite. Sykes Farm is to the right. The path is over grass and slabs of rock, just distinguishable on the ground, through another kissing gate to a post with arrows in the next field. Turn right towards "Keswick", then left at a field boundary, along the edge.

Follow yellow arrows to cross the Naddle beck on a wooden bridge and go straight across the next field to another bridge. Keep right, still following "Keswick", with a little rise ahead. Go through a farm gate and keep close to a wall, then a fence, on the right, to reach a stile and grassy path rising across the next field to the main road.

Turn right along the verge for 40 metres and turn right again at a farm access road with a public footpath sign; at a cattle grid turn left over a stile to rise a little further along over a worn grassy path. Join a surfaced farm access road beside a cattle grid Go straight through High Nest, passing close to the house, to a farm gate and continue along the track close to the wall on the right, with a potentially muddy section ahead.

Once again Blencathra is in front. The path is easy to follow over several ladder stiles. After the last stile aim towards the left edge of the plantation in front, where a gate gives access to the minor road. Turn left to return to the car park.

```
┌─────────────────────────────────────────────────────┐
│                                                       │
│           19. Thirlmere (north)                       │
│                                                       │
└─────────────────────────────────────────────────────┘
```

Length: 5 miles

Rise and Fall: Difficult to calculate, with much intermediate up and down. Between 500 and 550 feet (152 and 168 metres) in total, well spread. Only two sections are noticeably steep.

Underfoot: A variety of paths, some very good, others with stones and tree roots.

Car Parking: Signposted car park, (Swirls) with public conveniences, on the east side of the main A591. Grid reference 317169.

Map: Ordnance Survey Outdoor Leisure no. 5, The English Lakes, north eastern area, 1:25000 or Landranger no. 90, Penrith and Keswick, 1:50000.

Description

A walk especially recommended for lovers of lake side woodland, based on an accessible car park/picnic area close to a celebrated viewpoint. Whilst Thirlmere is unlikely to be anybody's favourite lake, the opening up of its surroundings by North West Water has allowed access to many excellent viewpoints and the lake need no longer be neglected, as it was for generations.

Manchester Corporation's much disputed take over of the valley and the creation of the reservoir in the 1890s resulted in a virtual no-go area for walkers. Obsessed by the need for water purity, the city fathers planted countless conifers in the most unimaginative way possible and denied all public access to a huge catchment area.

Thirlmere was, then, a place to be passed by on one or other of the valley roads, a sad hole in the heart of the district. Fortunately, more enlightened attitudes have prevailed in recent years and North West Water have not only provided several unobtrusive car parks close to the lake, but have also opened up footpaths and have carried out some works to assist walkers across boggy ground..

Near Thirlmere

Route

From the car park turn right and cross the main road to the parking area with views over the lake. Go down a few steps and through the kissing gate on the left, signposted "permissive path to Legburthwaite and Great How". A broad grassy path descends through the bracken towards the lake shore. To the left a beck noisily cascades in falls and rapids in its eagerness to slake Manchester's thirst.

Coniferous woodland is entered at a kissing gate with white arrow and the path swings right to follow the line of the lake shore. At times of low water, the unattractive "draw-down" area emphasises the importance of resisting the attempts which have been made in comparatively recent years to extend major water extraction to other lakes in the district.

Keep left at a fork and left again where a white arrow indicates departure from the broad trail. The woodland is now deciduous and is more attractive. After a kissing gate, a long disused launching ramp with rails may be noticed. Go straight on at a junction, through an area rich in brambles and nettles- walkers in shorts beware! Occasional white arrows and two kissing gates confirm the route

Bear right at a junction, away from the lake shore. In a short distance, after a left bend, comes a tricky bit of navigation. A very minor unsignposted path strikes off to the left, seven or eight yards after passing a beech tree by the track side on the left. Use of this path saves some distance and some ascent, but don't worry if it is missed; there is a perfectly good correction which can be made later.

The little path winds among the trees, not well used but never in doubt, to join a more major path in a quarter of a mile or so. (*If the path is missed, continue uphill to a four way signpost and turn left to head for the dam. The two routes soon come together*)

Great How summit is up to the right as the path heads for the dam at the foot of the lake, soon in view. Go through a kissing gate and down steps to the minor road which crosses the dam.

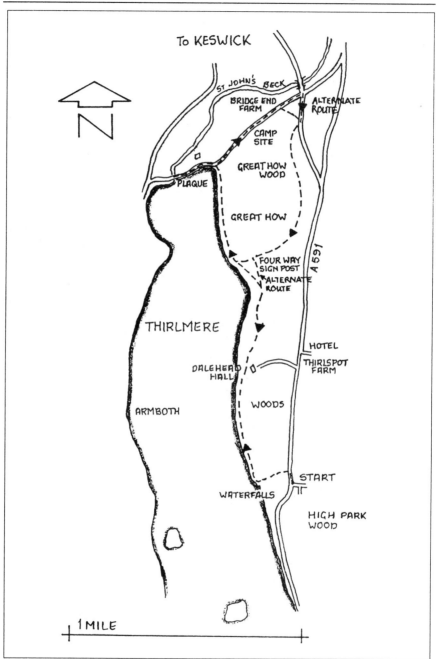

To KESWICK

N

ST JOHN'S BECK

BRIDGE END FARM

ALTERNATE ROUTE

CAMP SITE

GREAT HOW WOOD

PLAQUE

GREAT HOW

FOUR WAY SIGN POST

A 591

ALTERNATE ROUTE

THIRLMERE

HOTEL

THIRLSPOT FARM

DALEHEAD HALL

WOODS

ARMBOTH

START

WATERFALLS

HIGH PARK WOOD

1 MILE

Turn left along the top of the dam. The dominant element in the view is the great bulk of Helvellyn, but the lake itself is prettier than might be expected of a reservoir. To the right is a castellated waterworks building with the splendid coat of arms of the former Manchester Corporation – "Concilio et Labore". Next is the monumental plaque carved on a large slab of marble with the names of those involved in this considerable engineering achievement of more than 100 years ago.

Return along the road, passing a camping field and a small caravan site, then Bridge End Farm. Fifty yards before the main road turn right through the entrance gate of a bungalow and continue through a kissing gate labelled "permissive path". Climb a little through the woodland before descending to join a major track. (*The little climb can be avoided by staying with the road, turning right at the junction and entering the woodland at a kissing gate with signpost*).

A wide easy path now rises very slightly. Across the main road is Legburthwaite at the entrance to the Vale of St. John, with Castle Rock towering above. Visible ahead is the Thirlspot Inn at the foot of mighty Helvellyn. At the approach to a farm gate the track turns sharp right, rising more steeply for a short distance. As it levels out, the four way signpost is reached, completing the circumnavigation of Great How.

Turn left to head for the car park, re-using the outward route apart from the short cut along the minor path. Although this is a re-trace, care is needed at one or two forks in the path, helped by the occasional white arrow. The final ascent alongside the waterfalls to the viewpoint car park makes a rather strenuous finale to the walk.

20. Thirlmere (south)

Length: 1 1/2 miles.

Rise and Fall: About 130 feet (40 metres). No significant ascents.

Underfoot: Good, improved path by the lake side. Less well used but perfectly acceptable return.

Car Parking: Water Authority car park at Steel End, less than half a mile along the minor road from its junction with the main A591 at the south end of Thirlmere. Grid reference 321130.

Map: Ordnance Survey Outdoor Leisure no. 5, The English Lakes north eastern area, 1:25000 or Landranger no. 90, Penrith and Keswick, 1:50000.

Description

A very easy and simple walk for those with just a little time to spare or, perhaps, seeking to picnic by and/or explore the south end of Thirlmere reservoir. In recent times, spells of prolonged dry weather have exposed large areas of lake bed. Whilst less dramatic than similar exposure at Haweswater, this has aroused a fair amount of interest. Apart from the trim little 17th. century church, Wythburn hamlet, including two inns, disappeared at the time the reservoir filled in the 1890s.

Route

At the entrance to Steel End car park, a finger post points the way to Dob Gill, by a permissive path. Go through the gate at the far end of the car park and follow a well used path towards the lake. This is a very pleasant, easy path, with wooden walkways over streams and boggy ground. There are plenty of opportunities to divert to the right for a lake side picnic spot.

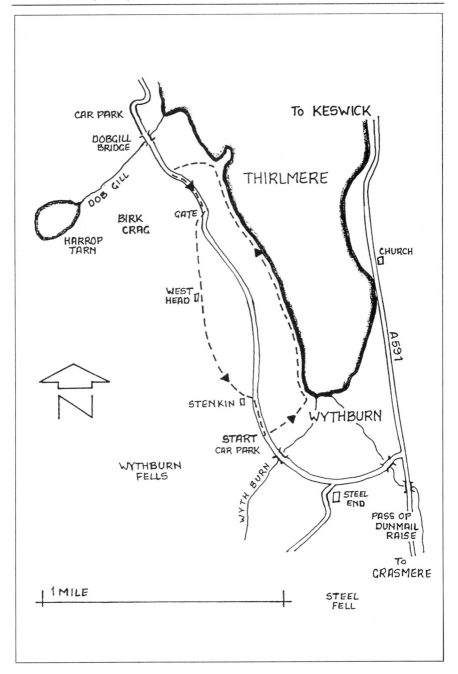

CAR PARK

DOBGILL
BRIDGE

To KESWICK

DOB GILL

THIRLMERE

BIRK
CRAG

GATE

HARROP
TARN

CHURCH

WEST
HEAD

A591

STENKIN

WYTHBURN

START
CAR PARK

WYTHBURN
FELLS

WYTH BURN

STEEL
END

PASS OF
DUNMAIL
RAISE

To
GRASMERE

1 MILE

STEEL
FELL

Wythburn Church

Inevitably, the view is dominated by Helvellyn, above to the right, but Wythburn church can also be seen across the water, having obviously just escaped the flooding which submerged the remains of most of the other local buildings.

The odd length of path would benefit from a trim of the rampant bramble and other undergrowth Turn right by a white arrow on a post, then left at a second arrow. Yet another white arrow is by a long collapsed ruin. Go between walls and fork left (faded white arrow on a tree) to rise to the minor road at a kissing gate. To the right Dob Gill races noisily towards the lake; the Dob Gill car park, with public conveniences, is a little further.

Turn left and walk along the road for 300 metres or so, with Steel Fell prominent ahead. Turn right at a gate signposted "bridleway to Watendlath" A grassy track rises to another gate. Go through and keep left along a built up track, not well worn but not difficult to follow, with a wall close on the left. The substantial ruins of a former farm and its outbuildings (West Head) with the inevitable fine crop of nettles, are passed before the path descends to farm buildings (Stenkin).

Pass through a gate to the left of the buildings to rejoin the road, Turn right to return to the car park.

21. Grisedale

Length: 5¼ miles

Rise and Fall: Between 400 and 450 feet (122 and 137 metres), largely in two sections, the longer being up the cul de sac road close to start. No really steep gradients.

Underfoot: Good easy footpaths and farm access roadways. No stiles.

Car Parking: Roadside spaces by the George Starkey Hut between Patterdale and Glenridding. Grid reference, 394161 or close to Patterdale church (2 hours limit).

Map:s Ordnance Survey Outdoor Leisure no. 5, The English Lakes, north eastern area, 1:25,000 or Landranger no. 90, Penrith and Keswick, 1:50,000.

Description

Grisedale (old Norse – Valley of the Pigs) is a substantial valley, smooth scraped by the glacial ice, separating the Helvellyn and Fairfield groups of mountains and carrying the long established pass between Patterdale and Grasmere. This straightforward walk allows a close approach to these fine fells without undue effort and gives views of some rugged rock scenery including hanging valleys (corries) such as Nethermost Cove.

On the northern valley side the well trod path to Striding Edge and Helvellyn climbs steeply, carrying its upward procession of those who know and those who don't know what excitement lies ahead on the airy traverse of the Edge. There are no special features in Grisedale; this is just a good walk up and down.

Nearby is Glenridding, formerly associated with extensive mining, a village with shops, hotels, the terminus of the Ullswater "steamer" service and other facilities. Patterdale is a smaller place,

Ullswater

more of a hamlet than a village, but with hotel, youth hostel and shop.

Between the two the parish church of St. Patrick is by the side of the road. Although the present church was consecrated only in 1853, this is an ancient site and the church has a font believed to be Norman.. There are interesting embroideries on the walls. Almost opposite the Glenridding boat landings is St. Patrick's Well, named in the locally held belief that St. Patrick preached and ministered to local people in this dale in the 5th. century, hence "Patterdale". There is, of course, no confirmation of this belief and Patrick may well have been a Norse/Irish settler of a much later date.

Route

Walk by the roadside towards Glenridding, passing St. Patrick's church. The peak in view ahead is Sheffield Pike. Turn left immediately before the road crosses Grisedale Beck into a surfaced cul de sac roadway, soon passing the entrance to Patterdale Hall. The road bends to the right quite steeply uphill, signposted

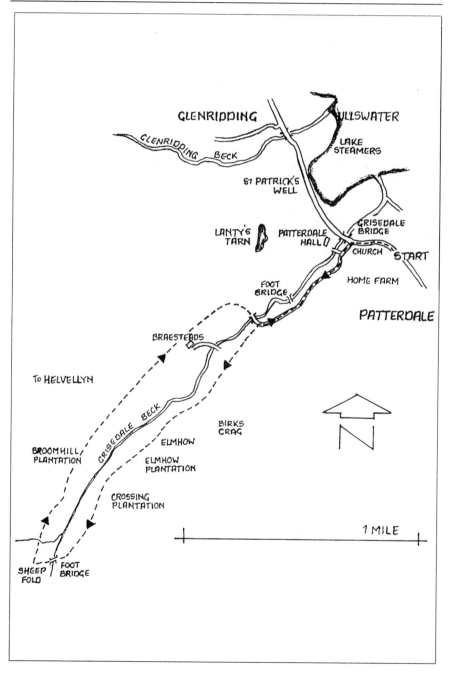

"Helvellyn via Striding Edge" The way levels out with the beck rushing along its deep wooded valley below.

At a junction go straight on through a kissing gate to continue along the Braesteads Farm access road. Leave this surfaced road as it turns right towards the farm and go straight on. To the right a shapely little stone bridge carries the road to the farm. The track is broad and very easy. Above to the left is the great bulk of St. Sunday Crag; across the valley is the ridge with the path leading up to the Hole in the Wall and the near end of Striding Edge. Pass the neat old farmstead of Elmhow and its adjacent plantation, with larch predominant.

At an isolated barn bear left to follow "Grisedale Tarn and Grasmere". A few gnarled old deciduous trees seem to emphasise the former bareness of this wild valley, softened in recent years by largely coniferous plantations, some of which do look rather artificial. The trees in a small, recent, linear plantation by the beck further upstream looked decidedly unhappy on a rugged January day.

Pass Crossing Plantation and, as the track begins to rise, fork right at a not very obvious junction, aiming for a broad wooden bridge over the beck, close by sheepfolds. Cross the beck, go through a gate in the wall beyond, and tackle the second ascent of the walk. A stony path rises to meet a more major path by a ruined building. There is a disused mine visible on the side of Eagle Crag above.

Turn right and follow the straightforward path, largely contouring along the hillside and passing above Broomhill Plantation and Braesteads Farm on its way back towards Patterdale. After about two miles, at a junction of paths, turn right through a gate to descend a steep little slope, reaching a surfaced roadway through another gate. Go straight ahead, cross the beck on a substantial stone bridge and rejoin the outward route. Turn left to return to the public road and the car parking area.

22. Hallin Fell, Ullswater

Length: 4 miles

Rise and Fall: Approximately 430 feet (131 metres), largely comprising the continuous ascent from Howtown to Martindale church. By the lake shore there are many short ups and downs.

Underfoot: Generally good paths and minor roads, but the path through Hallinhag Wood is rough underfoot, stony and with protruding tree roots.

Car Parking: The walk is written to start and finish by the public boat launching site near Howtown; grid reference 444198. However, parking space here is very limited and there is more space about one mile further along the road, by Martindale church; grid reference 435191. *If this latter car park is used, walkers not wanting to visit the steamer pier or Howtown hamlet can reduce the length of the walk by about half a mile by not descending the steps to Howtown Wyke but continuing along the path rising to the right to reach the road less than a quarter of a mile from the church.*

Map: Ordnance Survey Outdoor Leisure no. 5, The English Lakes, north eastern area, 1:25,000 or Landranger no. 90, Penrith and Keswick, 1:50,000.

Description

Howtown is definitely one of the Lake District's lesser settlements – a hotel, a couple of farmsteads, a steamer pier and a boat launching site. Additionally, its sole access by vehicle is along several miles of the very minor cul de sac road from Pooley Bridge to Martindale. In fact, were it not the mid lake calling point for the seasonal service of the lake "steamers", Howtown would be scarcely known to the majority of Lakeland visitors. Similarly, Sandwick hamlet and the little mountain of Hallin Fell are hardly listed among the great features of the district.

Having said all that, this is a lovely walk. The well rounded

Ullswater by Hallin Fell

shape of the fell lends itself well to circumnavigation and such a walk ensures constantly changing views to all points of the compass, with mountains, valleys, lake and woods all included. To circumnavigate a mountain is, of course, not an original idea. For example, each year many thousands of hardy walkers go all the way round Mont Blanc, climbing more than 25,000 feet (7620 metres) in total in seven or more days of hard walking. The present circumnavigation is more modest in its physical demands and can be completed in a couple of hours if so desired.

Route

From the launching ramp continue along the road for about 300 metres and turn left at the roadway into Howtown hamlet, signposted "Cote Farm". Pass the Howtown Hotel, with public bar, and rise through the hamlet. Stay with the road past an "authorised vehicles only" sign, soon close beside a rushing tumbling beck with a primitive stone bridge.

At a fork continue towards Cote Farm to reach a cattle grid and

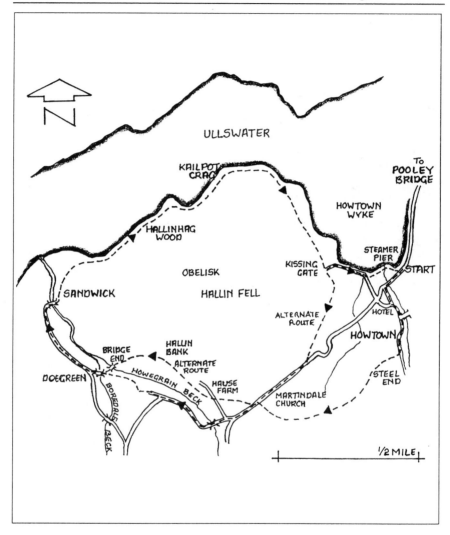

four way signpost. Turn right for "public bridleway, Martindale",
rising over close cropped grass to a well worn track. The views
to the left are up Fusedale, with part of the High Street range of
mountains beyond. After the initial rise the path levels to terrace
delightfully across the hillside, rising again towards its end. As
the path forks, go right, steeply uphill, before descending to
Martindale church. *From Howtown to the church the road may be*

used as a slightly shorter alternative if desired, also saving about 40 feet (12 metres) of ascent.

Turn left along the road, descending quite steeply. The glorious mountain views include the north eastern end of the great lump of Place Fell, carrying the names High Dodd and Sleet Fell on the Ordnance Survey map and, across Boredale, Beda Fell. Pass Hause Farm and keep right as the road forks. This road makes a good walking route but, *for those who hate all tarmac there is a path passing behind Hause Farm and contouring across the hillside past Hallin Bank before descending to Bridge End where the recommended route is rejoined.*

Drop steeply to the bridge over Howegrain Beck and stay with the road as it rises to the right up the valley side. As the road begins to level out in less than a quarter of a mile, fork right, slightly downhill to a roadway serving a house. Find a way past likely vehicular obstructions to a gate/stile just beyond the house. A grassy lane goes gently downhill. Turn right on joining a farm access roadway and continue along the bank of the beck, on tarmac. Pass Bridge End, cross Boredale Beck and rejoin the road.

Turn right towards Sandwick, descending a little. Gowbarrow Fell is the dominant height, facing across Ullswater. Follow the footpath sign "Howtown via Hallin lakeside path". Keep right along the road at the bottom to cross a bridge over Sandwick Beck.

A well used stony track now heads inevitably for the lake shore and what must be one of the best picnic spots in Lakeland. Woodland is entered at a kissing gate and the route is now entirely delightful as it rises and falls by the lake shore through Hallinhag Wood. However, the stony surface and the tree roots do require some care. The rocky Kailpot Crag is passed at the far end of the wood then the path swings right, now quite high above the shore of Howtown Wyke (Bay), with the steamer pier visible. At the foot of the lake Dunmallard Hill is the shapely height beside Pooley Bridge.

Turn left at a kissing gate and descend steps to head for Howtown pier and the boat launching ramp.

23. Pooley Bridge and Ullswater

Length: 2¼ miles

Rise and Fall: Negligible

Underfoot: Excellent tracks and three quarters of a mile on minor road.

Car Parking: Pay and display car park on the village side of the river at Pooley Bridge, grid reference 471244. Pooley Bridge is reached by a short diversion from the A592, Patterdale to Penrith road, right at the foot of Ullswater.

Map: Ordnance Survey Outdoor Leisure no. 5, The English Lakes, north eastern area, 1:25,000 or Landranger no. 90, Penrith and Keswick, 1:50,000.

Description

An entirely gentle little walk with the accolade of being the most level in this level walks book. The mountain setting of the head of Ullswater is superb, with Place Fell, Sheffield Pike and, above all, mighty Helvellyn all contributing to the scenic grandeur. The path alongside the lake is sheer delight with nothing to distract the walker from enjoyment of what is claimed by many to be England's most beautiful lake.

Pooley Bridge village is by no means a showpiece but it is a pleasant enough little place, with two inns, post office/stores. tourist information centre and public conveniences, strategically situated at the foot of the lake as the termination of the summer "steamer" service from Glenridding.

Eusemere is an impressive house with an even more impressive situation. It was built in the late 18th. century for Thomas Clarkson, the anti-slavery campaigner, and his wife, close friends of William and Dorothy Wordsworth who were frequent visitors. From Dorothy's Journals it is clear that the daffodils of the famous

Ullswater

poem were seen by William and Dorothy on 15th. April 1802, close by the water on the north side of the lake below Gowbarrow Park, as they were walking back to Grasmere after a stay at Eusemere. More recent owners of Eusemere include the late Lord Kagan, Harold Wilson's friend of "Gannex" raincoat fame.

Route

From the rear of the car park go through a small gate opening on to a lane and turn left. In a short distance keep left to take a surfaced driveway, with several large oak trees by the side, soon reaching the outbuildings of Eusemere. As the drive bends to the right, turn left through a gate with a "public bridleway" sign and cross a meadow angling towards a gate obvious on the far side. After an area trodden muddy by farm animals go through a kissing gate and turn right along the Pooley Bridge to Howtown road, generally quiet except, perhaps, on summer Sundays.

Pass Park Foot Country Club, Caravan and Camping Park, which offers a mini market and pony trekking, and reach Water-

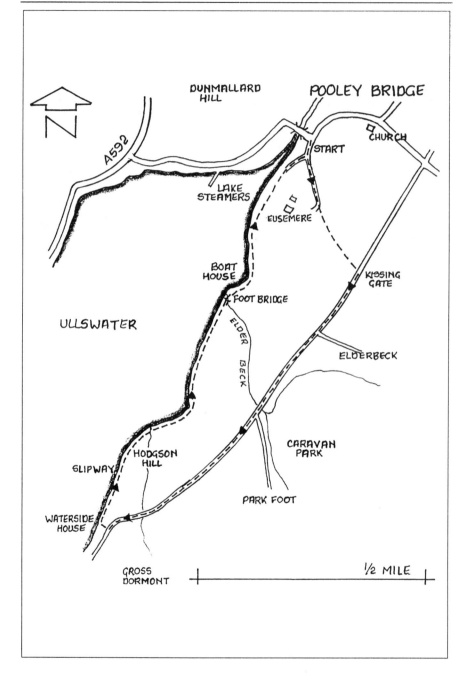

N

A592

DUNMALLARD
HILL

POOLEY BRIDGE

CHURCH

START

LAKE
STEAMERS

EUSEMERE

BOAT
HOUSE

FOOT BRIDGE

KISSING
GATE

ULLSWATER

ELDER BECK

ELDERBECK

CARAVAN
PARK

HODGSON
HILL

SLIPWAY

PARK FOOT

WATERSIDE
HOUSE

GROSS
DORMONT

½ MILE

side Farm in more than three quarters of a mile. Turn right at a public footpath sign, between farm buildings, to reach the lake shore, bending right, back towards Pooley Bridge.

Pass a camping field to reach a slipway where the venerable lake "steamers" (diesel since the 1930s) may be pulled from the water for winter laying up, repairs etc. Continue through a kissing gate beside the slipway and keep close to the lake shore. The path is always obvious, crossing a wet section on a board walk, passing a former boat house and crossing Elder Beck by a bridge. After a gate bear right then left to go along the top of a low bank, with Eusemere now in view.

The bridge at Pooley Bridge can be seen spanning the River Eamont as it leaves the lake before the track leads straight back to the little gate and the car park

```
┌────────────────────────────────────────────────────┐
│ ┌──────────────────────────────────────────────────┐ │
│ │                                                    │ │
│ │      24. Pooley Bridge, Dacre and                  │ │
│ │      Dalemain                                      │ │
│ │                                                    │ │
│ └──────────────────────────────────────────────────┘ │
└────────────────────────────────────────────────────┘
```

Length: 5¾ miles

Rise and Fall: Total of approximately 360 feet (110 metres), spread between five sections, none of which exceeds 100 feet (30 metres). None of the gradients are significantly steep.

Underfoot: Good – a mixture of farm tracks, grassy footpaths and the verge of a very minor road near Dacre. The return path by the River Eamont may be muddy in wet weather. Short lengths of the verge of the A592 road total about a quarter of a mile.

Car Parking: Choice of Lake District Planning Board pay and display car parks in Pooley Bridge. Grid reference (Dunmallard) 470245.

Map: Ordnance Survey Outdoor Leisure no. 5, English Lakes north eastern area. 1:25000 or Landranger no. 90, Penrith and Keswick, 1:50000

Description

A good, middle length, walk over predominantly low ground, linking Pooley Bridge, at the foot of Ullswater, with the old village of Dacre and the stately home of Dalemain.

Outside the rough, craggy, area of central Lakeland, which is determined by the rocks of the Borrowdale volcanic series, this is a landscape of more gentle rolling hills. Much younger sandstone and limestone are the geological base on which this attractive countryside is founded. Pooley Bridge is only a modest settlement by the foot of Dunmallard Hill, but it is provided with inns, tea room, shop, information centre, public conveniences and car parks. It is also the terminus of the "steamer" service from Glenridding, at the other end of the lake.

Dacre is a quiet, attractive, little village, with an inn and two important features. Firstly, St. Andrew's church claimed, on evidence from the Venerable Bede, to be on the site of an Anglo-Saxon monastery. The present structure was extended in the 13th. and 14th. centuries and then considerably restored, including rebuilding of the tower, in the 19th. century. Inside, there is a fragment of a carved 9th. century Anglian cross in a window and a 10th. century stone of the Viking period on the floor. The large lock of the south door is dated 1671 and is inscribed A.P. – Anne, Countess of Pembroke, better known as the legendary Lady Anne Clifford, whose steward Sir Edward Hasell later lived at nearby Dalemain.

In the churchyard are the famous Dacre bears (and cats) – four carved stone creatures by the corners of the church which tell some kind of story.

Dacre's second main feature is the castle, a 14th century pele tower designed to resist marauding Scots, on the site of an older fortification. Used as a private residence, the castle is not open

Dalemain

to the public, but the footpath passes sufficiently close to allow a good view.

The estate of Dalemain was purchased by Sir Edward Hasell in 1680 and is still owned by the same family. Most of the present elegant Georgian structure -the East front and the sides – dates from 1740-50, but the west range is much earlier, of the 15th./16th. centuries. During the season (broadly from early April to early October) the house and gardens and three small museums are open to the public on payment. Accessible without charge are a gift shop and licensed restaurant. Closed on Fridays and Saturdays.

Route

Set off along the broad track at the far end of the Dunmallard car park in Pooley Bridge, an inviting route close by the side of the River Eamont, below the wooded side of Dunmallard Hill. After a little more than a quarter of a mile, a fence is approached. Fifty metres before this fence, fork left to rise along a barely defined path which soon turns sharply towards the fence, reached at a gate and stile.

Go over the stile and turn left. Keep close to the fence for a quarter of a mile on a slightly vague footpath. The Helvellyn group of mountains comes into view to the far left as the shapely mound of nearby Dunmallard Hill is passed. The Penrith road is reached at a farm gate/stile. Go straight across to a kissing gate and "public bridleway" sign. The track is again a little faint on the ground, but keep the fence close on the left. Place Fell, by the head of Ullswater is now in view as the way rises towards a very minor road, passing a few huge trees on the field boundary.

By the roadside, just to the left, is the first of several iron seats in the Dacre area which commemorate the coronation in 1953. Turn right at the road and then left at a junction in less than a quarter of a mile, at a "Dacre ½m" signpost. After an initial slight rise, the road descends steeply to Low Bridge, crossing Dacre Beck. Wide verges make for good walking and there are soon views through the trees to Dacre Church and the nearby castle. Just after starting to descend, look out for an old boundary stone on the left, separating the ancient townships of Dacre and Soulby. In the bottom, before the bridge, is the Lord's Waste access area.

Cross the bridge and rise through the village towards the inn and the church. After seeking out the bears, return as far as the mini village green, which has a stone pillar with attachments, presumably a relic of the village stocks. A roadside signpost points to a "public footpath to Stainton", through a farm gate on the left as approached from the church. Go through the gate. The track forks at once. Keep right to pass close to Dacre Castle. The farm track continues unmistakably, generally straight and level, towards Dalemain. On a clear day the view ahead includes part of the distant Pennine Hills, on the far side of the Eden valley.

The Dalemain estate is entered beside a row of oak and poplar trees, the latter having considerably outgrown the former, with the stately house visible across the fields. A slight rise through woodland leads to the courtyard behind the house.

After any visit to the house, gardens, museums, gift shop, or refreshments, exit from the courtyard under the arch and turn right by the car park, and then bear left towards the main road. Turn right to walk to the bridge over Dacre Beck. About 60 metres to the right is an older bridge, presumably the original road bridge. Very obvious in this part of the Lake District is the sandstone which has, in addition to its fundamental contribution to the landscape, provided plentiful building material. Turn right immediately after crossing the bridge, over a stile.

The correct line is now to head for the near end of the old bridge, then turn left to aim for the left edge of Langfield Wood, nearly half a mile ahead across the huge rising field. Until fairly close to the wood, the path is not well defined on the grass. After passing the end of the woodland, the route becomes well marked, with pheasants in profusion, and fine views to Dunmallard Hill and the Helvellyn group. As the main road is approached, bend right and descend to the road over two stiles.

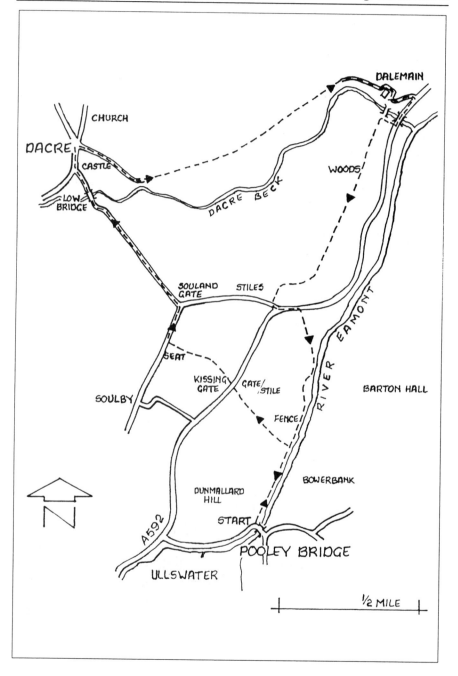

Turn left for a short distance and, as the road bends to the left, turn right at a signposted kissing gate. The likely mud on this section is largely avoided on walkways. Go left at a gate/stile, then to the right of an artificial pond, turning right at a kissing gate to reach the wooded bank of the River Eamont, along which an altogether gentle and attractive path heads straight back to the car park, rejoining the outward route on the way.

25. Askham and Lowther

Length: 3 miles

Rise and Fall: Approximately 270 feet (82 metres) in total, the great majority occurring in two separate ascents of the side of the valley of the River Lowther.

Underfoot: Very good throughout, with only the second ascent of the river bank potentially a little muddy and awkward.

Car Parking: Small informal area close to Askham church. Grid reference 518239. Askham is most easily reached by turning west along a minor road leaving the A6 half a mile north of Hackforth village.

Map: Ordnance Survey Outdoor Leisure no. 5, The English Lakes, north eastern area, 1:25,000 or Landranger no. 90, Penrith and Keswick, 1:50,000.

Description

This charming little walk is based on Askham, a village of great character with two large tree lined greens and plenty of cottages dating from the 17th. and 18th. centuries, all blending harmoniously. Facilities include two inns and a post office/stores.

Askham Hall, in private ownership, is tucked away behind a wall towards the bottom of the village but is to some extent visible from the line of this walk. Founded on a 14th. century fortified pele tower, the Hall was later converted into an Elizabethan mansion, with further re-modelling towards the end of the 17th. century.

Askham parish church of St. Peter, down by the River Lowther, was constructed in 1832 to the design of the architect of nearby Lowther Castle.

Despite its Gothic, fortified, appearance, Lowther Castle, on the site of an earlier castle, dates only from 1806-11. As the home of

Gardens Bridge

the celebrated Lowther family, it was constructed on a huge scale, the north front being 420 feet long. Unfortunately it was later abandoned for economic reasons and is now nothing more than an elegant but rather sad facade.

Much of the nearby chapel of St. Michael dates from the 12th. century, probably occupying the site of a much earlier church as evidenced by the 10th. century hogback stones in the porch. There have been many additions and modifications, most notably in the 13th. and 17th. centuries. Inside are many memorials to the Lowther family and other features such as a gallery formerly reserved for the family and a modern carving in the chancel. The site of this chapel was once within the village of Lowther, demolished by Sir John Lowther in the 17th. century and relocated half a mile or so to the east. Beside the chapel is a mausoleum of 1857 with a statue of one of the earls inside.

Route

Walk downhill to the road bridge across the R. Lowther. Turn right immediately after crossing and take either of the two invit-

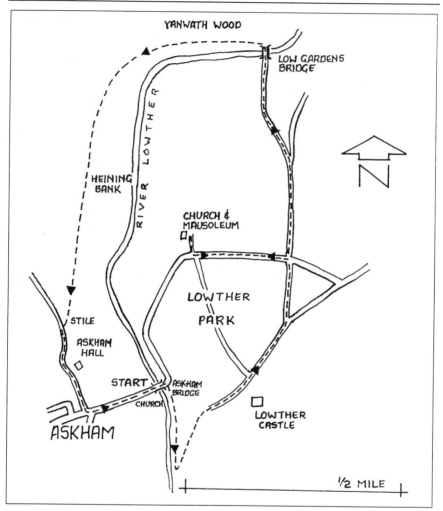

ing tracks through the attractive mixed woodland; that to the right is recommended for "level" walkers as it ascends the valley side at a more gentle gradient than the shorter route to the left. On the more gentle route join a wider track and turn sharply back to the left to rise towards the castle boundary wall.

Just after the reunion of the tracks turn right by the angle of the castle wall. Go over a cattle grid to enter a fine expanse of traditional parkland, with the chapel/mausoleum visible away to the left. By the castle gatehouse turn left, go through a farm gate and fork left in 120 metres. The best views of the castle facade are from this area.

At the public road turn left and follow the road for less than a quarter of a mile to visit the chapel/mausoleum, returning by the same route. Turn left along a surfaced roadway with a "public footpath" sign. As the road forks go left, downhill, towards the river where there are two bridges. Low Garden Bridge is a fine old high-arched stone structure, not now safe for vehicles. Beside is a functional utilitarian bridge. As a walker you may choose either bridge.

Immediately after crossing turn left, down the bank, to an old iron gate followed by another ascent of the river valley side, this time on a steep, possibly muddy, path through the woods, largely conifer with some rhododendron undergrowth. After levelling out the track continues along the top of the bank, passing fine mature pines and a plantation of spruce.

After a little more than half a mile from the bridge look out for a yellow arrow on a post to the right, just after a rack of fire beaters. Turn right to a ladder stile over a wall and go diagonally across a large field to a stile in the far corner, to the left of an obvious farm gate. There is no path apparent on the ground but there are views of Askham Hall. Over the stile turn left along an unsurfaced lane, passing some of the outbuildings to the Hall, to reach the road in Askham village towards the lower end of the main green. Turn left to return to your car, passing the Punch Bowl Inn.

26. Shap and Shap Abbey

Length: 3¼ miles

Rise and Fall: A little more than 200 feet (61 metres) in total, with the great majority comprising the fairly steep ascent of the side of the valley of the River Lowther.

Underfoot: Mostly very good lanes and footpaths. One overgrown section of lane.

Car Parking: Free car park with public conveniences by side of main road in Shap village. Adjacent to Memorial Park with bowling green and opposite Methodist church. Grid reference 564151.

Map: Ordnance Survey Outdoor Leisure no. 5, The English Lakes, north eastern area, 1:25,000 or Landranger no. 90, Penrith and Keswick, 1:50,000

Description

An undemanding circuit across upland farming country linking the village of Shap with the primitive chapel at Keld and the ruins of Shap Abbey. The route also passes some of the remaining stones of the prehistoric stone rows known as Shap Avenue.

Shap is very much a linear village strung along the A6 Kendal to Penrith road. Prior to the construction of the M6 motorway, it was a busy place, its inns and shops providing for the needs of the many travellers using this great highway to and from Scotland. From the mid 19th. century the name "Shap" has been universally known in railway circles, as it was applied to the steep and lengthy inclines leading to the English summit of the main Euston – Glasgow line of the London and North Western Railway, later the London, Midland and Scottish, although the actual summit is a few miles south of the village. The climb from the south was particularly notorious and, in the days of steam

Shap Abbey

locomotives, the locomotive depot at Tebay was kept busy in providing engines to bank the heaviest trains up the incline.

Although the railway line provides the eastern boundary of the village, it is now a comparatively quiet place. In open country, at an altitude of nearly 900 feet (274 metres), it is frequently cold and usually windswept.

Shap Abbey of St. Mary was founded early in the 13th. century by the Premonstratensian or "White Canons" Order, and was home to perhaps 12 or so of these brethren who ministered in surrounding parishes in addition to their monastic duties. Careful study of the ruins reveals various phases of the construction, with the 15th. century tower as the only substantial surviving part. Land holdings, both locally and further afield throughout Westmorland, were considerable. Dissolution came in 1540, since which date the structure has declined steadily, part being absorbed into a farm. It is now in the care of English Heritage and is open to the public without charge.

Keld chapel is probably of the late 15th. century and is an interesting example of an unrestored pre-reformation ecclesiastical building, with many original features including four of the five windows. The east window is similar to a window in the tower of Shap Abbey. The chapel was used for some years as a cottage, hence the fireplace, chimney breast and chimney. The roof is modern, following collapse of the original some years ago. The simply furnished chapel has been in the care of the National Trust for many years and is open to visitors. The key is kept at the house across the road, usually hanging in the porch. The chapel remains consecrated, a service being held in August each year.

Not very much remains of the avenue of stones generally known as Shap Avenue. Over the centuries the railway builders and local farmers have shown little respect for this late Neolithic/early Bronze age monument. Most obvious is the Goggleby Stone, re-erected in a concrete box after a fall in modern times but some others can also still be seen.

Route

Turn left along the main road for a little more than 100 metres. Turn right at a public footpath sign to go through a farm gate. Angle left in 20 metres through another gate, with yellow arrow.

A fairly clear path over short grass keeps close to the limestone wall on the right. One or two of the stones of Shap Avenue may be seen. Go over a stile and bear right along an obvious path. In the middle of the meadow, as the path bends to the right, turn left along a lesser path leading to a stile over the wall. Go over two more stiles within a short distance, then a third to reach an old unsurfaced lane. Turn left towards farm buildings. 100 metres short of the buildings turn right into a similar lane. This is wide open rough upland farming country with just a few improved pastures showing a brighter green colour. In view ahead are the flanks of the hills and mountains around Swindale and Haweswater.

Go through a farm gate and descend gently towards Thornship, a sizeable farmstead. After a right bend the way past the farm is obvious, joining the surfaced access road. Continue to Keld hamlet. The primitive chapel is in the angle at the road junction.

From the chapel go uphill along the road for less than 100 metres. Turn left over a cattle grid at a signpost "Footpath. Shap Abbey" and go along the upper edge of the garden of a newish house. Go over a stile and continue along the edge of a rough meadow. At a junction of paths at the end of the wall keep straight on. Climb over the wall on the left at a high and rather awkward stile, turning right to continue the same line to a stile over the wall ahead.

The not well defined route is now just above a narrow strip of woodland with the River Lowther below. The Abbey suddenly comes into view. After a stile/gate turn left down a steep bank, rough underfoot or carry on a little further to the surfaced road serving the Abbey and turn sharp left. In either case cross the bridge to reach the Abbey.

From the Abbey take the surfaced access road to climb quite

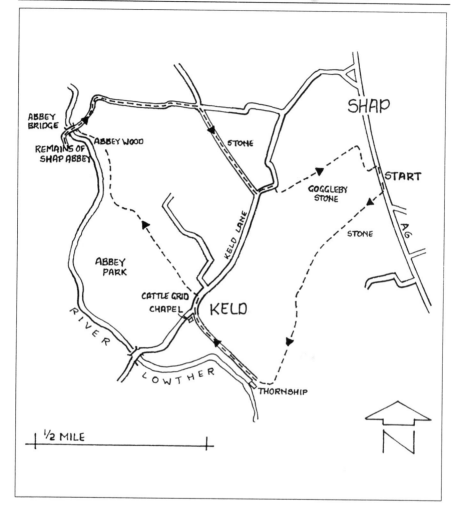

steeply up the valley side to a cattle grid with a stile beside. Here a choice may be made between continuing along the very quiet road or going over the stile to follow a right of way along the edge of the field. The routes stay close together and end at the same place.

Join the public highway and turn right at once into a narrow lane signposted "Keld Lane" There is some tree, shrub and nettle obstruction of this lane but carry on regardless. Shap village is visible to the left. Turn left at the public road (Keld Lane) and, in 100 metres, turn right into another unsurfaced lane. Turn left in 40 metres over an arrowed stile.

Ahead is the Goggleby Stone; another of the ancient stones can be seen on the left, close to a wall. The path back to Shap is now very clear, along the field edge, over two stiles, up a small rise and heading straight for the church. Go through a gate into the built up area. Turn right along a back lane and then left to the main road. Turn right to return to the car park.

27. Blencathra Centre and Skiddaw House

Length: a) 5¾ miles; b) 6½ miles; c) 8¼ miles

Rise and Fall: a) 630 feet (194 metres); b) 550 feet (169 metres); c) 975 feet (300 metres)

Underfoot: Splendid footpaths throughout, largely terraced across grassy hillsides.

Car Parking: Small free car park just beyond the Blencathra Centre, accessed by a cul de sac road climbing from the middle of Threlkeld village. Grid reference 303256.

Maps: Ordnance Survey Outdoor Leisure no. 4, The English Lakes, north western area, 1:25,000 or Landranger no. 90, Penrith and Keswick, 1:50,000.

Description

Unusually in a book devoted to circular walks, the basic walk suggested here is an out and back excursion to Skiddaw House. Variation b) requires the use of two vehicles or an obliging non-walking driver prepared to meet the walkers at the car park at the end of the cul de sac road reached from Ormathwaite or Applethwaite, just to the north of Keswick. Variation c) is a longer walk reverting to the normal circular format, but at the expense of a total ascent considerably greater than is usual in a "level" walks book.

The route is at a comparatively high level on the flank of Blease Fell, part of Blencathra ("Saddleback") and there are fine views to the south and south west over the Vale of Keswick to the group of fells which includes Grisedale Pike, Causey Pike and Catbells, and to the Helvellyn range.

The valley of the Glenderaterra Beck separates Blencathra from the eastern slopes of the Skiddaw massif, this end having the name Lonscale Fell. Although there are minor crags on the Skiddaw side, the valley is generally gentle in its contours, typical

By the Blencathra Centre

of Skiddaw slate countryside in contrast to the more dramatic Borrowdale Volcanic series rocks just a few miles to the south. For walkers this means that the footpaths on either side of the valley are gently graded, following the contours of the valley sides in easy terraces. Even the final rise to Skiddaw House is nowhere steep.

Skiddaw House has a remarkable situation, right in the middle of nowhere. It has for many years been used as a youth hostel. The remoteness presumably guarantees its popularity with those hostellers who still regard arrival and departure at a hostel on their own two feet, carrying equipment in a rucksack, as the proper way to travel.

The variation walks provide even more of the splendid views, with an excellent return route for those opting for the full circuit, (c).

Route

Take the broad inviting track which rises gently from the car park, soon bending right to head north up the Glenderaterra valley. No navigation is necessary for more than one mile. Eventually, close to the valley head, a descent is made to a footbridge over the beck.

Ascend to a junction of ways near a sheep fold. Turn right here to continue rising to Skiddaw House, one mile further. Return by the same route.

For variations (b) and (c) turn left at the junction of paths to head south along another fine terraced path on the west side of the valley. The path bears right around the end of Lonscale Fell before crossing the little valley of Whit Beck to reach the car park which is used by walkers ascending Skiddaw by the popular Jenkins Hill path.

For variation (c) turn left from the Skiddaw car park to follow a broad track heading for the right hand edge of a belt of woodland. Stay with this track as it descends towards the wooded valley of the Glenderaterra Beck. Before reaching Brundholme

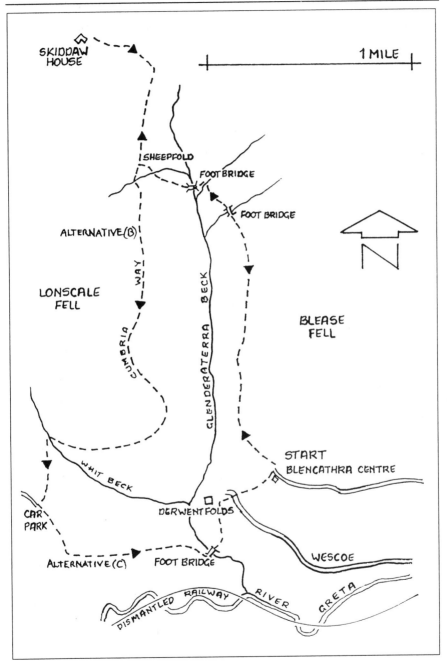

look out for a rake back which eases the gradient down the steep side of this attractive little valley.

Cross the beck by a footbridge and start the steady ascent back to the Blencathra Centre, which has been visible for some distance. A well used track rises to the former farmstead of Derwentfolds. Turn right here and shortly cross a lane to a signposted footpath leading directly back to the Centre. Follow the indicated route through the buildings to the roadway above. Turn left back to the car park.

More Lakeland walking guides from:

WALKING
LAKELAND TRACKWAYS:
the Eastern Lakes
Mike Cresswell
£6.95

**COUNTRY WALKS IN THE
HOWGILLS**
Mary Welsh
£6.95

**COUNTRY WALKS AROUND
KENDAL**
Mary Welsh
£6.95

**NORTH LAKELAND WALKS WITH
CHILDREN**
Mary Welsh
£6.95

**SOUTH LAKELAND WALKS WITH
CHILDREN**
Nick Lambert
£6.95

**TEA SHOP WALKS IN THE LAKE
DISTRICT**
Jean Patefield
£6.95

**THE LAKELAND SUMMITS: a
survey of the fells of the Lake
District National Park**
Tim Synge
£7.95

FULL DAYS ON THE LAKELAND FELLS:
25 challenging walks in the Lake District
Adrian Dixon
£7.95

STROLLING WITH STEAM:
Walks along the Keswick Railway
Jan Darrall
£4.95

100 LAKE DISTRICT HILL WALKS
Gordon Brown
£7.95

LAKELAND WALKING: on the level
Norman Buckley
£6.95

MOSTLY DOWNHILL: Leisurely Walks in the Lake District
Alan Pears
£6.95

LAKELAND ROCKY RAMBLES:
Geology beneath your feet
Bryan Lynas
£9.95

PUB WALKS IN THE LAKE DISTRICT
Neil Coates
£6.95

TOWN & VILLAGE DISCOVERY TRAILS: Cumbria & The Lake District
Norman Buckley
£6.95

In case of difficulty, or for a free catalogue, please contact: **SIGMA LEISURE, 1 SOUTH OAK LANE, WILMSLOW, CHESHIRE SK9 6AR.** Phone: 01625-531035; Fax: 01625-536800. E-mail: sigma.press@zetnet.co.uk . Web site: http//www.sigmapress.co.uk

ACCESS and VISA orders welcome. Please add £2 p&p to all orders.